Spells for Money and Wealth

Angela Kaelin

2012
Winter Tempest Books

ISBN-10: 0615718035
ISBN-13: 978-0615718033
Winter Tempest Books

DEDICATION

In memory of my grandparents.

CONTENTS

i

1 ABOUT SPELLS FOR MONEY AND WEALTH

Spells are more than just thoughts or wishes. While these things may play a role, there is a procedure to conducting spells, which involves gathering and focusing directed psychic energy, followed by a controlled release. Of course, conducting any kind of spell doesn't guarantee the desired outcome of a situation, but it may influence it.

Spells for money and wealth are similar to other kinds of spells in that they are conducted mainly to affect your environment and the other people in it, however, they have an added value in helping you to achieve a more positive attitude toward your own prosperity. They can, also, help you to feel more confident in your interactions with others with whom you do business and help you to enjoy the fruits of your labor.

Spell casting is a universal practice, which is why you will find ideas from many different cultures and traditions in this book. It includes a basic formulary for magical oils, powders, incense and washes, which are used in these spells and may be incorporated into any magical working for money and wealth.

Use the spells and formulas in this book whenever you want to draw money, pay your bills, overcome debt, apply for a job or solve financial problems. Conduct these spells to live a life of comfort, enjoy good luck in games of chance, reverse bad fortune and attract good fortune.

How Money Spells Help You to Achieve a Healthier Prosperity Consciousness

The concept of prosperity consciousness has risen to widespread public awareness in the past several years. It has its roots in the writings of New Thought authors from the late 19th and early 20th centuries and involves a fusion of ideas from Christianity, Theosophy, hypnosis and the power of positive thinking cult.

While some modern spiritual and marketing gurus have over-simplified the methods of altering prosperity consciousness, even taking the concepts to dangerous extremes, the main idea behind developing and maintaining a healthy prosperity consciousness has merit.

It is not unreasonable to suggest that your thoughts, including subconscious ones that may have been planted during your early childhood, may have an effect on your present attitude toward the acceptance of prosperity.

Unless your parents were very wealthy, you probably grew up hearing such platitudes as "Money doesn't grow on trees" or "Life is hard and then you die." You might have been called lazy by one of your parents or told that you would never amount to anything. Sometimes these words motivate people, but they may, also, set up a subconscious cycle of failure or cause people focus so hard on earning money that they forget how to relax and enjoy the rewards of their resulting wealth.

Even if you did not subconsciously receive these ideas at home, it is still likely that you were taught something similar at school. After all, the educational system is set up to create a large subset of the population who are programmed to earn money and perpetuate the economic system. The most educated among us often end up as cogs in the machinery of corporate slavery, which is not always a path to either money or wealth.

Yet, the conditioning to this idea is so deep that most people will balk at the suggestion that any reasonable alternative exists. Such people are in a mental prison without even realizing it. This is so because it is inter-generational conditioning, perpetuated by the system in place and often by parents who were conditioned to this same thinking just as their parents were.

Once you awaken to the idea that your prosperity consciousness may be flawed in some way, you can begin to do work on a subconscious level to improve it. If you fail to remove the emotional attachment you have to these old ideas, they may continue to sabotage all your best efforts to prosper.

All spells affect the mind and emotions of the spell caster to some extent, even when they are worked with the intention of only influencing external circumstances. But, many of the spells in this book function as a method of re-wiring the subconscious to accept prosperity. Certain spells included here are designed to purge adversarial influences before you begin working on other money spells.

Money spells, also, help you to prepare yourself psychologically for greater prosperity, particularly if you are in sales or if you run a business of your own. They can be used to generate courage and confidence, inspire your creativity and increase your business intuition. Spells for wealth help you to shift your mindset from that of a workaholic to a more relaxed one where you are able enjoy the fruits your hard work produces.

How Money Spells Influence the Environment

Money spells are a means of consciously directing accumulated energy by means of the emanations from your own mind in order to create a desired effect in the environment. For example, if your overall surroundings are not conducive to money drawing and the establishment of wealth, you can cast spells to influence the elements in your surroundings to become more favorable to your endeavors.

It would be nice to believe that just your thoughts or your own efforts alone are all that is necessary to achieve success, but this is simply not how the world works. While success at accumulating money and wealth may be somewhat dependent on the efforts of the individual, the fact is that no one succeeds without help from others. In fact, the people who go furthest in life are often not the hardest workers, but those who are able to make the right social connections. If you were not born with a silver spoon in your mouth and you lack a well-placed benefactor, spells for money and wealth may help to arrange things in your favor.

Another important factor in achieving almost anything in life is luck. Many people do not believe in luck, either good or bad, however, if you observe the pattern of your life, you will probably see that it is a little bit like a casino. Sometimes you are a high roller and sometimes you go on a losing streak. Many successful people admit that while hard work may have been a factor in their success they, also, had good luck or they were in the right place at the right time.

Also, by means of magic, you may be able to heighten your intuition and creativity so that you make better decisions about your business and career and are better able to position yourself to make the right social connections. Moreover, if your energy is strong and properly focused and directed, you may be able to influence important people in your favor.

Since the world is full of abundance, you should never fear being greedy or selfish in your spell work. Don't be too humble. Ask for more than what you need to merely eke out a living. The more abundance you have in your own life, the more you will have the time, the means and the opportunity to reach out and help others in need.

Believe in your own goodness and work your spells for money and wealth with confidence. Even if you don't succeed the first time, you will be working to rewire your subconscious mind and re-tune your prosperity consciousness.

What is the Difference Between Money and Wealth?

For the sake of simplicity, when we talk about money, we often mean a host of other things to do with prosperity including wealth, careers and success in other aspects of life. But, money is really only one aspect of prosperity.

Money is a medium of exchange, whereas wealth is a state of being in which you have the things you need and desire. Wealth refers to all the things money can buy, including land, precious metals, nutritious food and other necessities. It has a strong relationship to success in other aspects of life that may interest you, such as family and career. Wealth is the state of having all of the things you want and need in life, whereas money is only a means of acquiring them, however, this is where most of us must put our attention first.

If you are trying to meet your monthly expenses, you need money. After you have accomplished this, accumulating wealth is the next level. Once you have enough money to meet your basic needs, then think about using the excess to accumulate wealth and create a lifestyle of comfort and luxury for yourself. Wealth is about expansion and doing all of the wonderful things with your life you want to do without being overly committed to the worker mentality, which can get in the way of your enjoyment of the fruits of your labor.

Never feel guilty about wanting to lead the comfortable lifestyle you are entitled to it. When you accumulate more money than you need to simply survive, you are able to do more than just work for a living and are better able to realize your full potential as a human being.

The Use of Coins in Spells

Have you ever worked a money spell using paper currency, like the dollar bill, and had it fail miserably or backfire?

This may be because the U.S. dollar, which is a medium of exchange, is, also, a note of debt to the U.S. Treasury. In the U.K., a similar system exists involving the Bank of England. These paper bills are often not the best choice to use in spells for drawing money or wealth. Using them in spells to acquire more money or to erase debt may backfire and create more debt.

Just as a Federal Reserve debt note has a vibration of debt attached to it, precious metals like silver and gold have wealth vibrations attached to them. For this reason, silver and gold coins are often the best choices to use in spells for drawing money and wealth. An exception to the rule is the two-dollar bill, which is regarded as good luck, especially if it is fresh from a bank or minted in a leap year. If you decide to use paper money in your spells, this bill is the best choice.

Many spells in this book make use of coins, particularly those made of silver, copper and gold, which are noble metals. If you don't already have some, coins comprised of 90% silver may be purchased from coin shops fairly inexpensively. In the American Hoodoo tradition, Mercury Head dimes, especially those minted during a leap year, are considered to be the most powerful. Copper coins are abundant and may be used when unspecified coins are called for. Gold coins are more expensive, so they are recommended less often. But, they are extremely powerful, especially in spells for success and wealth. If you have them, you should use them in your spells.

2 TIMING OF SPELLS FOR MONEY AND WEALTH

To maximize the efficacy of your spells, choose an auspicious day and hour. If you do not adhere to this rule, your spells will not necessarily fail, however, you may have more success if you begin your spells at the right time. The following information should be considered as a guideline.

Timing plays a role in many aspects of life on this planet, such as planting and harvesting. So, it is no wonder that spell casting is affected by timing in a similar way. The old alchemists noted that certain experiments failed at certain times and succeeded at others, although they were not always sure why. In the same way, you should approach the timing of your spell casting as an experiment.

Some spells in this book give specific times which are most propitious for their performance. Whenever timing is not specified, spells for money and wealth are best conducted during a full or waxing moon or on a Thursday, Friday or Sunday. The exception is spells to banish debt or disharmonious spirits and thought forms, which are best performed during a dark or waning moon.

When in doubt about timing, you may generally rely on these times as good choices. Although, there are specific days, which may be more beneficial depending on the exact nature of your intention.

Tuesday is the day of Mars, which is the planet of power and aggression. Spells for competitive businesses, sales and management or any situations that require you to dominate other people are ideally conducted on a Tuesday or when the Sun or Moon is in Mars and its energy is expanding.

Thursday is the day of Thor and Jupiter. It is associated with expansion and growth. Thursday or when the Sun or Moon is in Jupiter are beneficial times for conducting spells for money, business, growth and increase, as well as for opening offices or other places of business and for beginning new enterprises.

Friday is associated with the planet Venus, as well as the old Germanic god and goddess Frey and Freya, who are associated with prosperity and abundance. Therefore, Friday or when the Sun or Moon is in Venus is a favorable time to conduct spells involving the expansion and growth of your existing career or business plans and the acquisition of money.

Sunday is associated with the Sun, which smiles upon all endeavors begun on this day and crowns them with the laurel of success. Sunday is ideal for conducting spells for careers, success and wealth.

The Sun, Moon or Jupiter in Capricorn is, also, a good time for working spells for material wealth.

By contrast, Saturday is generally avoided for conducting spells for domination, success, money and wealth because it is associated with decrease and a contraction of forces.

The minutes after sunrise on any day are the most powerful time to perform spells associated with the influences of that day.

Days of the Week

Sunday (Sun): Success; fame; illumination; learning; vitality; family; dealing with authority figures and court cases.

Monday (Moon): The home; meditation; prophetic dreams; planting and harvesting and affecting time.

Tuesday (Mars): Passion; vigor; aggression; courage; adventure; the triumph of the will; success in military actions; law suits; conflicts; sports and conquering.

Wednesday (Mercury): Communications; higher learning; occult studies; business; acting; the arts; sales and marketing; writing; short trips; deception and con artistry.

Thursday (Jupiter): Prosperity; abundance; growth; expansion; increase; optimism; increased earning; good luck; healing; psychic development and expansion of awareness; investments; settling disputes and giving blessings.

Friday (Venus): Love; friendship; other affairs of the heart; charity; social situations; parties; gatherings; weddings; engagements; romance; beauty and communications with women.

Saturday (Saturn): Binding; shrinking; restricting; decreasing; marriages; contracts; legal matters; to break a habit; chronic illnesses; older people; the dark arts; cursing; hexing; hex breaking; revenge and spell reversal.

Moon Phases

As a general rule, if you want to attract something to you, conduct your spell when the moon is full. If you want to get rid of something, do your spell when the moon is waning.

New Moon: This phase begins the first day of the new moon and lasts for 3 1/2 days. It is a good time to conduct spells for new businesses and new jobs. This is the best phase during which to open a new place of business.

Waxing Moon: This phase begins 7 days after the new moon and lasts for 7 days. It is the right time to conduct spells to attract wealth and increase money and prosperity, to gain something you want, to foster friendships, to improve health, wealth, luck, love and success.

Full Moon: This phase begins 14 days after the new moon and lasts for 3 1/2 days. It is a good time to conduct spells for divination, protection, legal matters, financial improvement, growth, abundance and increased energy.

Waning Moon: This phase begins 3 1/2 days after the full moon and lasts for 10 1/2 days. It is the right time to conduct spells involving the dark arts, to bind, for revenge, to break a habit or addiction and to banish a problem.

Dark of the Moon: This phase begins 10 1/2 days after the full moon and lasts for 3 1/2 days. It is a good time to conduct spells for banishing, separation, revenge and to stop theft.

The Moon in Beneficial Astrological Signs

Another way to determine the best time to conduct spells for money and wealth is based on the characteristics of the moon in the twelve signs of the zodiac. Almanacs give the signs of the moon throughout the calendar year and some web sites offer "Moon Sign Calculators" you can use to determine the position of the moon for any day of the year.

Beneficial aspects of the moon for conducting spells for money and wealth are as follows:

Moon in Aries: Spells for money; to get a job; increase sales; improve business; for strength; courage and passion.

Moon in Taurus: Spells for practical, every day matters.

Moon in Gemini: Spells related to communication and healing.

Moon in Cancer: Spells involving the home and increase.

Moon in Leo: Spells for fame; career; and success.

Moon in Virgo: Spells revolving around learning; healing; security and stability.

Moon in Libra: Spells pertaining to contracts; legal matters; marriages; court cases; partnerships and peace-keeping.

Moon in Scorpio: Spells pertaining to divination; spiritual communication; the dark arts; psychic enhancement and sex-related matters.

Moon in Sagittarius: Spells involving travel and learning. Avoid doing spells for divination or psychic enhancement at this time.

Moon in Capricorn: Spells for domination; control and stability.

Moon in Aquarius: Spells for healing; peace; harmony and understanding.

Moon in Pisces: Spells for divination; astral travel; spirit communication and emotions.

Some practitioners, also, choose odd numbered hours of the day to conduct spells because they are regarded as more powerful than even numbered ones. Multiples of three are regarded by some as especially powerful.

Spells do not necessarily fail if your timing is imperfect, however, proper timing may provide the natural energy flow favorable to the outcome of your endeavor. If a spell fails at one time, try it again at another time and it may work very well.

Angela Kaelin

3 HERBS AND MINERALS
FOR MONEY AND WEALTH

Use the following herbs in your spells, potions and charms for money and wealth:

Abre Camino (Eupatorium villosum or Koanophyllon villosum): Road opener
Alfalfa: Good luck and to prevent poverty
Allspice: Good luck; success in business and for money gained through business ventures
Alkanet: Purification; money; prosperity; success in business and gambling
Almond: Money and prosperity
Allspice: Good luck; prosperity; courage and success in business
Aloe Vera: To expel evil; protection of home and business
Amber (Ambergris): Courage; long life; success; strength; inspiration; psychic powers and wealth
Angelica: To reverse bad luck; destroy negativity and impart creativity and inspiration
Anise: Youthfulness; divination; psychic ability; protection from the evil eye; good luck and gambling
Ash Bark: Prosperity and protection
Bayberry: Money; wealth and seeking employment

Basil: Money; wealth; protection and success in business

Bay Leaves: Job success; promotions and pay raises

Benzoin: Steady flow of money; steady employment and confidence

Bistort (Snakeweed): Money; wealth; fertility and to increase psychic powers

Bergamot: Confidence and to command and control others

Bladderwrack: Protection; money; psychic powers and safe travel

Black-eyed Peas: Money and good luck in the coming year when eaten on New Year's Day

Black Snakeroot: Love; lust and wealth

Bluebonnet: Good luck and gambling

Blue Flag: Money

Buckthorn: Court cases; contracts; legal matters; wishes; protection and exorcism

Cabbage: Good luck

Cactus: Protection and seeking employment

Calamus (Sweet Flag): To dominate a person or situation

Calendula: To win in court; luck in the lottery and prophetic dreams

Camellia: Love and luxurious wealth

Cashew: Money and prosperity

Cassia Leaf (Cinnamon): Luck and money

Chamomile: Good luck; money and wealth

China Berry: Good luck and to make changes

Cinnamon (bark): Power; lust; aphrodisiac; fast money and to increase the action of any potion

Cinchona: Protection and good luck

Citronella: Money; fast luck; to draw customers and success in business

Cloves: Money; wealth; banishing and protection from evil

Coltsfoot: Money and wealth

Coconut: Purification; protection; good luck and good health. Coconut is the "Tree of Life."

Dandelion: To draw good luck to your home or business (bury the root at the four corners)

Devil's Shoestring: Protection; power; stop gossip; gambling; good luck and employment

Dill: Love; lust; money; wealth and protection
Dock: Money; fertility and healing
Dragon's Blood: Love; gambling; confidence and to restore sex drive in men
Fenugreek: Prosperity; to get a raise; luck with money and wealth
Five-Finger Grass (Cinquefoil): Money; wealth; gambling; to gain favors and creative inspiration
Flax: Money; protection; beauty; physical health; mental health and increased psychic powers
Fumitory: Money and exorcism
Garlic: Protection of the home; exorcism; lust and to prevent theft
Ginger: Money; love; power; protection; gambling; success and restful sleep
Ginseng: Beauty; increased energy; love; lust; good wishes and protection
Gold of Pleasure (Camelina or False Flax): Wealth; growth and abundance
Golden Seal: Money and powerful healing
Gorse: Money and protection
Grains of Paradise: Money; good luck; wishes and inspiration
Grapes: Money; fertility and wishes
Gravel Root: Seeking employment
Harebell: Prosperity and opening up the consciousness to the possibility of wealth
Heliotrope: Prophetic dreams; visions; wealth; invisibility and exorcism
Hickory: Court cases; contracts and legal matters
High John the Conqueror (Ipomoea Jalapa): Domination; money drawing and gambling
Holly: Money; good luck; powerful dreams; honesty; protection from lightning strike and all evil
Honeysuckle: Love; money; prosperity; increased psychic powers and success in business
Horse Chestnut: Money; healing and increased circulation
Hyacinth: Love; protection; peace and good business
Hyssop: Purification; protection and jinx breaking

Iris: Wisdom; courage and to bless infants

Irish Moss: Money; good luck and protection

Jasmine: Money; wealth; creative inspiration and to attract customers

Jezebel Root: Dark arts; hexing; cursing; money and achievement

Job's Tears: Good luck; gambling and to make wishes come true

Juniper Berries: Love; good luck; wealth; success in business; exorcism and protection from thieves

Larch: Protection from thieves

Lemon Balm (Melissa Officinalis): Love and success

Lemon Verbena: Love; good luck; purification and to increase the potency of any potion

Lemongrass (Cymbopogon): Lust; psychic powers and to repel snakes

Low John (Galangal root): Money; wealth; protection; to break hexes and to drive away bad luck

Lungwort: Safe air travel and as an offering to spirits of air

Mallow: Love; protection and exorcism

Mandrake (European): Love; wealth; protection; growth and increase. (Poison. Do not ingest)

Maple: Love; lust; money and longevity

Marigold: Protection; legal matters; psychic abilities; visions and dreams

May Apple (American Mandrake): Money

Mints (Spearmint, Peppermint, etc): Good luck and to attract helpful spirits

Mistletoe: Love; fertility; breaking hexes; exorcism and a successful hunt (Poison. Do not ingest.)

Moonwort: Love and wealth

Moss: Money and good luck

Mustard Seed: Gambling; protection from the evil eye; exorcism and increased mental powers

Myrtle: Love; fertility; youthfulness; money and peace

Night Jasmine (Cestrum nocturnum Has No Hana, Hasna Hena): Good luck and gambling

Norfolk Island Pine (Araucaria heterophylla): Protection from evil and poverty
Nutmeg: Money; good luck and gambling
Nuts: Fertility; harmony and prosperity
Oak: Money; good luck; fertility; potency; exorcism; protection and court cases
Oats: Money
Onion: Money; prophesy; lust; exorcism and to speed the recovery of strength after severe trauma
Orange: Love; luck; money; gambling; insight; meditation; divination and happiness
Osha Root (Ligusticum Poteri): Purification and good luck
Palmarosa: Purification and good luck
Papaya: Love; protection and digestion
Patchouli: Money; wealth; protection and wishes
Pea: Love and money
Peach: Love; fertility; longevity; exorcism and wishes
Pecan: Money and steady employment
Periwinkle: Love; lust; money; wealth; protection and wishes
Pine Needles: Money; protection; cleansing; fertility and exorcism
Pomegranate: Fertility; divination; good luck; wishes and wealth
Poplar Bark: Money and air travel
Poppy Seed: Love; persuasion; wealth; fertility; invisibility and relief from insomnia
Purslane: Recovery of debt and protection from psychic attack
Ragged Robin: Purification and to remove obstacles
Raspberry (leaves): Protection; good luck and gambling
Rattlesnake Plantain (Goodyera Oblongifolia): Carried as a good luck charm.
Rattle Snake Root: Protection from sudden death and accidents (Carry in a purple flannel bag.)
Rice: Money; fertility and to bring rain
Rose of Jericho (Anastatica): Money, good luck and prosperity

Rose: Love; healing; good luck; glamor; courage; protection and to increase psychic powers

Rowan: Protection; power; success; psychic powers and healing

Rue (Ruda or Ruta Graveolens): Money; good luck; protection and hex breaking

Salep (Lucky Hand): Money; good luck; gambling; employment; protection and safe travel

Skullcap: Money and wealth

Smart Weed: Money and wealth

Sarsaparilla: Love and wealth

Sassafras: Money and good health

Sea Holly: Achievement and to destroy obstacles

Sesame: Lust and wealth

Skullcap: Money; wealth; love; fidelity and peace

Smart Weed: Money and wealth

Snakeroot: Good luck; money; gambling; protection and health

Spikenard (Nardostachys Jatmansi): Love; money; protection and strength

Squill Root: Money and wealth

Strawberry Leaves: Good luck

Sulfur: Hex breaking; protection and to break someone's control over another person

Sumbul: Love; good luck; psychic powers and good health

Sunflower: Wisdom; fertility; health and wishes

Tea: Wealth; strength and courage

Thyme: Love; divination; psychic abilities; sleep; purification; courage and money

Tonka Beans: Good luck in business

Vanilla: Good luck and to quicken the action of any spell

Vervain: Money; peace and protection

Vetivert (Khus Khus): Love; good luck; protection and peaceful harmony

Wheat (Wheatgrass): Money and fertility

White Peony (Paeonia Lactiflora): Protection and exorcism

Wintergreen: Good luck and protection

Winter's Bark: Success

Wisteria: Anointing; meditation; channeling; mental concentration and feminine sexuality
Wood Rose: Good luck
Woodruff: Money; protection and success
Yellow Evening Primrose (Primula Vulgaris): A successful hunt

Crystal Gemstones for Attracting Money and Wealth

In general, money-drawing stones can be recognized by their green or golden colors, however, each stone is known for its specific powers, as follows:

Abalone: Protection in business
African Jade: Good luck and wealth
Agate: Good luck and gambling
Alabaster: Drawing and attracting whatever you desire
Amazonite: Success; confidence and good luck in gambling
Amber: Protection; good luck; gambling and wealth
Ametrine: Overcoming procrastination and fear
Atlantasite: To make good financial decisions and to succeed in business through your own efforts
Black Obsidian: Protection; money and vision (Used as a medium of exchange by the ancient Aztecs)
Bloodstone: Money; success in business; prosperity consciousness and invisibility during travel
Carnelian: Calm focus; to inspire successful action and to overcome the fear of public speaking
Chiastolite: Protection for travelers and to increase the power of other prosperity stones
Chrysoprase: Good luck and wealth
Cinnabar: Wealth (Keep this stone with your money.)
Citrine: Success; to attract good customers and maintain wealth. (It is called the "Merchant's Stone.")
Cymophane (Cat's Eye): Wealth; protection from the evil eye and to return lost money or items
Emerald: Money; wealth; to increase sales and to promote public awareness of a business

Fire Opal: Good luck; money; power; protection from the evil eye and to acquire powerful friends

Fluorite: Creativity and to build wealth (This stone is especially good for women.)

Green Aventurine: Money; good luck; gambling and the lottery

Green Calcite: Money and wealth

Green Garnet: Money and good luck

Green Tourmaline: Money; wealth and beneficial contracts

Iolite: To eliminate debt

Jade: Wealth; good luck; setting and achieving goals; longevity and a fulfilling life

Jadeite: Strength; stamina and protection from fatigue

Jet: Protection of self and finances

Lepidolite: Stress reduction; inspires independence and independent achievement

Lodestone: To attract what you desire (Generally; you need two, which must be fed iron filings.)

Malachite: Wealth and success in business; to accomplish goals and to open the road to success

Moldavite: Wealth; success; inspiration; opportunities and the shedding of old ideas and constructs

Moonstone: Transitions and heightened intuition

Moss Agate: Money; to find hidden treasure and to acquire powerful friends

Mother-of-Pearl: Money and wealth

Nephrite: Success; transitions and protection from misfortune

Pearl: Protection from bad investments and unnecessary financial risks; good luck and gambling

Peridot: Money; wealth; to attract opportunities and formulate a clear vision of the future

Pyrite: Money; good luck; gambling and wealth

Pyromorphite: Wealth

Red Garnet: Wealth and success in business and career

Ruby: To make sound financial decisions

Sunstone: Assertiveness and to improve self-esteem

Tiger's Eye: Money; wealth; good luck and inspiration

Topaz: Wealth and opportunities
Turquoise: Wealth; good luck; travel and moving from one place to another
Zircon (Red or Purple): Wealth and protection from thieves

4 FORMULARY OF OILS, INCENSE, POWDERS AND WASHES

Many of the potions listed in the formulary below may be purchased from metaphysical shops, however, you can easily make them yourself. The potions you make are likely to be far more powerful than any you can purchase because you have control over the quality and quantity of the ingredients and they will be charged with your own energy and intentions. Use the same timing for potion-making as you would use for conducting spells based on your purpose.

To make a powder from any of these formulas, combine and pulverize the herbs listed in the recipe in dried form using a coarse mortar and pestle or an inexpensive coffee grinder. When amounts are not specified, use equal parts of each herb in the formula.

Powders may be sprinkled around your home or place of business and used in mojo bags or charm bags. They may, also, be burned as incense, either with or without a piece of charcoal. When using charcoal discs, always use an appropriate burner on a surface that can absorb heat because charcoal becomes extremely hot. Always follow the directions on your charcoal incense burner tube.

To make an oil from any of these formulas, you can

proceed in one of two ways:

(1) Combine the dried, powdered form of the herbs with a base oil, such as Almond, Safflower or Sunflower. In a glass jar, combine approximately one part of the herb mixture with two parts of oil. Tighten the lid down securely on the jar. Then, allow this to sit for, at least, two weeks in a warm place. Shake the jar twice per day. After two weeks, strain the oil into a dark glass bottle using cheesecloth or a strainer and label it accordingly.

(2) Combine a few drops of each essential oil of the herb in the formula into about a cup of base oil. Essential oils may be purchased at metaphysical stores, botanicas, health food stores and online.

To create a house wash using any of these formulas, combine the herbs and boil them in approximately one quart of pure water. Allow the potion to cool. Then, strain it and use the liquid as a wash to scrub the floors, walls, porch and sidewalk of your home or business.

To make a ritual bath, place several drops of the essential oils in a formula into your bath water.

To make a wash suitable for the house or a bath, combine the essential oils in a formula with unscented Castille soap. Dilute this soap to make the wash suitable for nearly any surface that can be cleaned.

To make bath salts, combine Sea Salt with powdered herbs or essential oils. Mix and crush them using a mortar and pestle.

Oil formulas may be applied to your clothes or to mojo bags and used to strengthen your other spells.

Take care applying certain oils to your skin, particularly if you are sensitive or prone to allergies. For example, Cinnamon oil may burn your skin if it is not well-diluted with a carrier oil. Some oils, especially, citrus essential oils should not be applied to skin that may be exposed to sunlight because they may cause changes in skin pigmentation. If you are pregnant or nursing, take special care not to apply some essential oils to your skin. Essential oils should never be used on infants or cats.

As you create your potions, meditate on their purpose

and direct their power with your words. Ask for spiritual guidance and use your intuition. If you feel the formula could benefit from a pinch of another herb, like those listed in the previous chapter, follow your intuition.

Store your potions in dark glass bottles with airtight lids away from heat and light. Label and date each one as you complete it.

Never ingest these formulas.

Algiers
For love and luck in gambling

Cinnamon
Orris root
Patchouli
Vanilla bean

Better Business #1

2 parts Irish Moss
2 parts Vetivert
1 part Gold or silver magnetic sand
1 part Frankincense

Better Business #2

Mix and pulverize equal parts of the following:

Allspice
Anise
Basil
Bay
Cinnamon
Frankincense
Myrrh
Rose
Tonka Bean
Vetivert

Black Cat Oil
To reverse bad luck and attract good luck

1 cup Almond oil
1 T. Angelica root
2 T. Chamomile
1 T. Rose Geranium
1 T. St. John's Wort
2 T. Solomon's Seal

If you are a gambler, this is one of the lucky oils you rub on your hands before rolling the dice.

Drawing
To attract good spirits and good luck

Jasmine
Lavender
Violet

Fast Luck

Cloves
Ginger
Gum Mastic
Lemon peel
Orange peel

Gambling

Allspice
Heather
High John the Conqueror
Patchouli
Pine resin

Generosity

Lavender
Orris
Sage

Sprinkle this oil or powder near the entryway of your business where customers and prospects must walk through it.

Get a Job
Imparts luck, domination and courage

Black Pepper
Clove
Ginger
Gravel Root
Lavender
Rose
Ylang-Ylang

Get a Raise

Allspice
Bayberry
Bay Leaves
Couch Grass
Dragon's Blood
Fenugreek Seed
Gravel Root.

Good Luck #1

Jasmine
Myrrh

Good Luck #2

Jasmine
Myrrh
Rue
Wintergreen

Good Luck #3

4 parts Catnip
1 part Cinquefoil (Five Finger Grass)
4 parts Lavender
1 part Marjoram

High John the Conqueror Oil
To dominate and succeed in gambling,
all financial matters and court cases

2 to 3 parts Almond oil
1 part High John the Conqueror root (powdered)

It is difficult to find High John the Conqueror essential oil. Therefore, use the above formula to make your own oil infusion. Pulverize the root and place it in a jar with the oil. Keep it in a warm place away from direct sunlight for two weeks. Strain the root out and bottle the liquid. Place a whole root in the master bottle.

Many magical High John the Conqueror formulas purchased from magical suppliers contain other ingredients besides High John. You may follow this example by adding several drops of Dragon's Blood or Myrrh oil to enhance to power of this potion.

Job Hunting
For success in getting the next contract,
gig or employment situation

Gravel Root
Mistletoe

Sea Salt
Woodruff
Yellow Evening Primrose

Luck in Court Oil

3 drops Geranium
3 drops Lavender
3 drops Verbena
1 oz. Jockey Club

This formula is derived from information given in Zora Neale Hurston's book *Mules and Men*.[1] A formula for traditional Jockey Club is given in Chapter 11 of this book.

Money Drawing

Bayberry
Eucalyptus
Marjoram
Pine
Rue
Sandalwood
Spearmint

Prosperity

Allspice
Basil
Bayberry
Coltsfoot
Honeysuckle
Magnolia
Patchouli
Pine

Red Carpet
For when you want V.I.P. treatment

Iron Weed
Marigold blossoms
Plumeria blossoms
Red Rose petals

When making Red Carpet Oil, place a piece of Pyrite or Fire Opal in the master bottle.

Red Fast Luck Oil
For luck and to draw customers to your business

Cinnamon oil
Vanilla oil
Wintergreen oil

Combine equal parts of the above. Add a small amount of base oil. This potion is based on Red Fast Luck given by Zora Neale Hurston in *Mules and Men*.[2]

Reverse Bad Luck

Clove
Copal
Dragon's Blood
Garlic
Rue
Sandalwood

Road Opener Oil
To destroy obstacles and pave the way to success in any endeavor

1/2 cup Almond oil
9 drops Citronella oil
3 drops Cinnamon oil
9 drops Cedar oil
9 drops High John the Conqueror Oil
9 drops Palmarosa oil
9 drops Vanilla oil

Place a High John the Conqueror root in the master bottle.

Road Opener Powder
Use this powder in Road Opener spells when your efforts seem blocked

Abre Camino
Blue Bonnet
Cedar
Cinnamon
High John the Conqueror
Lemongrass
Nutmeg
Sandalwood

Safe and Prosperous Business Travel

Basil
Bayberry
Calamus Root
Comfrey
Lungwort
Plantain
Salep

Sales Oil

1/4 cup Almond oil
3 drops Bay oil
3 drops Bayberry oil
3 drops Cinnamon oil
3 drops Jasmine oil
3 drops Sandalwood oil

Steady Work #1

Bayberry
Benzoin
Clover
Gravel Root
Rose
Sea Salt

Steady Work #2

Bayberry
Benzoin
Gravel Root
Sea Salt

Success in All Endeavors Oil

1/2 cup Almond oil
7 drops Amber oil
7 drops Bay Leaf oil
7 drops Juniper oil
7 drops Lemon Balm oil
7 drops Myrrh

Success in Business #1

Bayberry
Cedar
Cinnamon
Lilac Blooms
Pine
Sandalwood
Spearmint
Vanilla
Violet

Success in Business #2

Anise
Bergamot
Cinnamon
Geranium
Lavender
Orange Blossom
Rosemary
Wintergreen

Super Fast Luck

Basil
Cinnamon
Patchouli
Peppermint
Pine Needles
Vanilla
Wintergreen

Van Van Oil #1

In American Hoodoo, Van Van is used to attract good luck and to increase the power of any other potion or working. This is a very versatile formula, which is often used as a base or an additional ingredient to other formulas and is helpful in cases where you want to speed the action of a formula or you feel some obstacle may be in your path.

This particular formula is loosely based on one described by Catherine Yronwode (www.luckymojo.com).

1/2 cup of Almond oil
16 drops Lemongrass oil
8 drops Citronella oil
1 drop Vetivert oil
1 drop Palmarosa oil
1 drop Ginger Grass oil

You may also add a few small pieces of Pyrite to the mixture. Use Van Van to dress Lodestones and talismans. Van Van is protective and helps clear the way for opportunities in your life.

Van Van Oil #2

In *Mules and Men* by Zora Neale Hurston, Van Van oil is described as nothing more than Lemongrass oil in alcohol. Proportions are not given. Despite this, some researchers assert that the term, "Van Van," is a corruption of "Vervain" and that this is the main ingredient.

Wealthy Way
For all the luxuries money can buy

Allspice
Angelica
Cinquefoil (Five Finger Grass)
Frankincense
Jasmine
Myrrh
Nutmeg
Spearmint
Vanilla
White Lotus oil

You will find more formulas throughout this book within descriptions of spells. A more complete formulary including aspects of timing, incantation and making substitutions is given in the *Traditional Witches' Formulary and Potion-making Guide: Recipes for Magical Oils, Powders and Other Potions* by Sophia diGregorio.

5 HOW TO CHARGE OBJECTS

A spell book is really little more than a recipe book. It can tell you which items to use, what words to say and when to conduct a procedure, but there is an important element that only the spell caster can supply to the operation. This is your own condensed and focused psychic energy.

No spell book can tell you everything you need to know to make a spell work because the real power comes from within. This is a power derived from both knowledge and practice of the art and science of magic, which involves controlling the elements and applying mental force or *will* to them.

The objects used in spells should be charged with the elemental forces. There are four primary elements: Fire; air; water and earth.

When we speak of elements in this way, we are not referring to actual fire and water, but to esoteric concepts that possess similar qualities. The terms, fire, air, water and earth, are not to be taken literally. Although, they are sometimes used symbolically in spells or rituals, it is only to remind practitioners of these esoteric concepts and not to create a worship or reverence for physical nature.

The two main elements you must concern yourself with

for the purpose of charging objects are fire and water. Within every atom and within you, two principle forces are at work, one is electronic and fiery and the other is magnetic and watery in nature. These elements are called fire and water respectively and refer to the electromagnetic force within all of nature, including the metaphysical world. Here, again, nature does not refer to the great outdoors, but to the universal construct as a whole.

It is these two elements that create a powerful force within you which you can direct in order to gather more energy and charge objects. It has unlimited other uses, as well, but within the scope of this book, we will only discuss its use in spell casting.

Before you can charge an object, you must gather the elemental forces.

How to Gather Energy

The two elementary forces, fire and water, are similar to the properties in a battery. One has a positive charge and the other one has a negative charge. This charge is not only magnetic, it is, also, a wave form. The fiery principle repels and exerts force in an outward motion, whereas the watery principle, attracts and exerts a magnetizing force in an inward motion. This repelling and attracting, in and out motion is the nature of the electromagnetic force.

It is necessary for you to be able to quiet your mind and focus for just a few minutes at a time to charge an object. Relax yourself by taking a couple of deep breaths and releasing the tension from your body.

Put your mental focus on the place inside your body located on your spine and behind your navel. With each breath, pull the element of fire, the active component of electromagnetic energy, out of the environment and form it into a little ball in the pit of your stomach.

Keep growing this energetic ball with each breath, which you will see as a ball of bright, white light, slightly tinged with a vibrant shade of red. Continue growing this ball and condensing its power until you have dense accumulation of it.

Then, while holding this ball there in the pit of your stomach, begin to accumulate the water element from the environment around you. Add it to the existing dense ball. This energy is tinged with blue and green and it swirls around like smoke as you gather it out of the air and pull it into the ball of energy. Do this until you have a more or less equal amount of fire and water element gathered together in this ball.

The air element exists naturally as a force of equilibrium between the elements of fire and water. You do not need to make a conscious effort to include it.

After you have accumulated a dense ball of fire and water that you are satisfied with, draw in a little bit of earthy, dark red and gold energy to bring the vibratory level down just slightly. This helps to make the energy more dense and physical.

This is how you gather electromagnetic energy. Using your imagination, you can now cause the ball of energy to disperse and go down into the ground. Or, you may continue with the operation of charging.

How to Charge Any Object

Place before you the object you want to charge, whether it is a candle, a potion you've created, a glass of water, a talisman or any other object you might use in a spell.

Close your eyes for a moment and imagine the entire world as nothing more than a sea of vibrating energy. Become aware of the infinite matrix of tiny spinning atoms. Now, focus your attention on just one of these atoms and project your conscious awareness into the center of it. What you find there is an electromagnetic force, which is tinged by the nature of whatever thing it is a part of.

It is on this subatomic level that you will be projecting your energy into objects. These objects function as multidimensional holograms and like holograms, if you affect one part of it, you affect the entire thing.

You may open your eyes or keep them closed while charging an object. Hold the object to be charged or place your hands over and around it. In your mind, see this item on its atomic level as a collection of vibrating atoms. By the force of your will, cause the ball of energy you accumulated to move through your body, out of your hands and finger tips into the center of the atoms that comprise the object. Alternatively, you may project it straight out of your abdomen by means of a visualization in which it simply pours directly out of you and fills the form of the object before you.

Once this is done, the object is energized with the electromagnetic elements of fire and water. You must now project your mental powers upon the energy in the object and impregnate it with your will or intention.

Suppose, for example, that you want to charge a candle, which you plan to burn as part of a spell to find the perfect job for you. You will be burning this candle, which will probably be green to represent your desire for money and increase. The smoke from this candle, which is its essence, will be carried into the outer environment to impregnate the energy around it with your desires.

Begin by filling yourself with energy as previously instructed. Then, direct the accumulated energy into the object. With your mind's eye, see the energy filling first one atom, then every atom of the candle. Once you have filled the object completely, impress your desires (your will) upon the vibrating force you have placed within it.

You may do this by speaking to the object as if it were a person. Say, "Now, you shall become an instrument for my will. You are to find and return to me the money and wealth that I desire." You may, also, use a formal incantation or only the force of your thoughts.

Once you have done this, you may end with the word, "Amen," or the phrase, "So mote it be," or whatever words of power you might want to add to this procedure. Your object is now fully charged with your focused energy and impregnated with your intention by the force of your will.

How to Make and Charge a Talisman

A talisman is an object you carry with you, usually under your clothes and touching your skin, which is empowered with specific energies intended to attract or repel a certain condition.

Some types of talismans are made of engraved metal and are widely available from metaphysical stores and jewelry-makers. The Seal of Jupiter from old grimoires like the "Greater Key of Solomon" is an example of such a talisman. The beneficial astrological influences of the planet Jupiter are magnified through the use of this talisman. Jupiter is associated with success, money and power in the world. Its influence is one of expansion, growth and greatness.

Jupiter talismans have specific methods of construction and consecration applied to them to increase their power. These procedures differ, but are outlined in grimoires like Francis Barrett's *The Magus*, Henry Cornelius Agrippa's *Three Books of Occult Philosophy* or *Key of Solomon*. Generally, the talisman is constructed of tin or pewter, which contains tin. It is best made and consecrated on a Thursday at sunrise.

To do this, the magician faces east and invokes the planetary powers of Jupiter. This helps to charge it. Then recite your incantation. An incantation from the *Greater Key of Solomon* is given here is to be used as an example:

The Oration

"O ADONAI, most Holy, Most Righteous, and most Mighty God, Who hast made all things through Thy Mercy and Righteousness wherewith Thou art filled, grant unto us that we may be found worthy that this Experiment may be found consecrated and perfect, so that the Light may issue from Thy Most Holy Seat, O ADONAI, which may obtain for us favor and love. Amen."

This grimoire instructs the magician to, then, place the talisman in clean silk and bury it for twenty-four hours at the junction of a crossroad. Afterward, the talisman's power can be called upon by placing it in your right hand and whenever you wish to obtain grace or favor from someone, your wish will not be denied. The energy of the talisman is fed by passing it through the smoke of incense or by anointing it.

Magic squares or kameas are a type of talisman that incorporates numerology. They are drawn on parchment or paper and carried by the magician. Runes and other symbols are used to make a variety of talismans for different purposes that can be charged and kept with your money, used in spells or placed into a mojo bag with your selected herbs and stones.

A mojo bag is another type of talisman, which can be customized. Design your own personalized money, wealth or good luck drawing talisman by acquiring or making a little red or green, flannel draw-string bag about 3" x 5" and filling it with stones and herbs, which possess the energies you want to bring into your life. Instead of a flannel bag, you may use a linen or cotton handkerchief and tie it with a ribbon or cord.

For example, if you want to create a talisman for success in business, combine Fluorite, Red or Green Garnet, Basil, Allspice, Juniper berries and Grains of Paradise into a mojo bag and anoint the herbs in the bag with Success in Business Oil.

Alternatively, you might choose to use herbs from one of the formulas in the previous chapter to design a mojo bag. For example, if you want to create a mojo bag to draw money, place the herbs from the Money Drawing formula (Bayberry, Eucalyptus, Marjoram, Pine, Rue, Sandalwood and Spearmint) into a mojo bag.

If you must travel for your work, then you might add a piece of Turquoise and a Bloodstone for protection during travel as well as good luck and money drawing.

If your job requires that you have some authority or influence over others, then you might want to add a whole, unbroken High John the Conqueror root to your bag. Direct the power of the High John the Conqueror root for a specific purpose by anointing it with a particular oil such as Calamus root for added domination power plus good luck and protection or Rue oil for enhanced money drawing through domination.

A whole High John the Conqueror root is often used alone as a talisman, particularly for luck at gambling and in any case where you want to dominate a situation or other people. As a talisman, it is anointed for a specific purpose. For example, a gambler anoints it with Gambling Oil, then places it in his or her pocket to be touched before rolling the dice.

Regardless of what type of talisman you choose, it must be fed from time to time by being anointed or passed through incense, specific to your objective. When you anoint or feed your talisman, don't just go through the motions of rubbing on the oil or waving it through the cascade of incense smoke, but gather your energy and pour it into the object, then impregnate that energy with the force of your will.

Sympathetic Magic

Most spells make use of what is called sympathetic magic. This is the occult science of correspondences or similarities between objects. What is at work here is the "Law of Similars," which is used in homeopathy.

It means that we can use things of a similar vibration to create an influence. We find objects that have a vibrational frequency similar to the type of action we want to bring to bear and we manipulate and exert that force on objects that are vibrationally similar to that which we wish to influence. This is why we make use of plants, minerals or other object that have properties similar to the influences we want to bring to a working.

Effigies, poppets or "voodoo" dolls are dressed with items that are similar to the influences we want to imbue them with. They are usually associated with a particular person by means of that person's personal effects, which carry his or her vibration, such as a photograph, blood, hair, nail clippings and other personal items.

For example, if you wanted to influence your boss to give you a promotion at work, you would obtain something that has his vibrational signature on it. This might be a photograph, nail clippings or a piece of paper the person has signed his name on. You might conduct your spell using a doll or a candle to represent the boss and include the item with his similar vibration to it.

To get a promotion, you would act upon this vibratory representation of your boss in a way that represents what you want to happen in the physical world. You would influence his personal vibratory rate from a distance using powders, oils and other substances that impart energies that correspond to your purpose.

You might do something to symbolize your domination of the boss in this matter. You might even use your own blood or other bodily fluids together with a success or domination potion. If you combine a few drops of your own blood with this oil, you create a potion that has both your vibrational signature combined with a vibration of success and domination.

Afterward, you would apply this potion to the image, candle or other object that carries the boss' similar vibration, charge the objects concerned with your energy and impregnate that energy with your will, as previously described.

In this way, you are distantly influencing your boss' mind and emotions by imposing these sympathetic energies and your will upon an object that carries a similar energetic signature to his own. When you act upon an object that represents a person's energetic vibration, it as if you are acting upon the actual person.

Understanding the Theory Underlying
Successful Spell Casting

To get the most out of your efforts, it helps to understand the basic magical theory behind spell casting.

Every spell should be conducted with the most energy

you can conjure and direct into the operation. After you have put a great deal of energy into your spell, you must release it. Essentially, this is done by emitting either a burst or a sustained flow of energy, then afterward forgetting about the entire issue. This is why you are frequently instructed to bury an object or place it somewhere to be forgotten.

Specific herbs, minerals and other objects are employed in spells because of their innate energy. For example, silver coins actually contain silver, which is real wealth and some herbs and gemstones contain a vibration similar to an energy you want to work with for attracting abundance.

If you apply this similar energy to an object that has the same or similar energy to the object you are trying to affect, for example, yourself, your business or your home, then you are affecting one energetic form by another through sympathetic magic. Distance healing, also, works on the same principles. So, does distance harming.

This same principle is elegantly stated by Aleister Crowley in the famous quote, "Love is the law, love under will." Love means resonance, harmony or an energy with a quality similar to that you want to work with. Love under will is a reference to manipulating this energy with your mind.

So, the process of performing any magical working involves the following:

1. A clearly defined objective

2. The target to be acted upon or its representative

3. Harmonic similarity or resonance with the action you want to produce through the use of candles, herbs, gemstones, coins, colors, etc.

4. Charged intention, directed by the mind or the will upon the objects employed in the spell

5. A final, complete release of this energy

This final step is important. Once a spell has been performed, if the energy involved is held onto by the spell caster, it will never have the opportunity to work. Your will must be released into the outer environment to influence the universal vibrational field. In many spells it is released through burning and allowing the essence of the charge to be carried through the air, liquid being poured out into the earth, or the refuse of the spell is buried or hidden.

The Value of Secrecy

Silence is golden. Speaking of something draws upon its energy and causes others to do the same. This is why it is wise to keep silent about your spell work not only during the performance of an operation, but afterward.

Fortunately, the average person's thought emanations are not very powerful and the biggest problem you might have with them is being subjected to ridicule or being thought insane. The main danger is from other witches and magicians whose trained minds might adversely influence or steal some of the energy from your spell.

So, unless you are working with another like-minded person to conduct a spell, do it alone and keep silent about it. Don't even whisper about it to yourself.

Another aspect of secrecy and power exists in the customization of spells and making them your own. Customizing the spells in this books will give your workings further insulation against psychic intrusion from others, which might take power away from them.

The more you perform spells and work with the ideas of sympathetic magic, energetic gathering, charging, willing and releasing, you will naturally develop your own ways of doing things within the bounds of the laws of occult science. There is more on the concept of creating spells through sympathetic magic and charging objects in the book, *How to Write Your Own Spells for any Purpose and Make Them Work*, by Sophia diGregorio.

6 CLEARING SPACE AND PREPARING TO WORK

Places sometimes accumulate psychic energy, which may either be a help or a hindrance to your endeavors depending upon its nature. Energetic emanations, whether your own or those of others, even those who might have lived or worked in a place a long time ago, may accumulate and work against your attempts to draw money and wealth into your life. It is important to cleanse such vibrations from your home or place of business before you begin to create a more positive energetic environment.

If you are experiencing bad luck or you feel that your home or business environment is not as positive and success affirming as you would like, you may want to consider conducting a simple cleansing.

To attract more harmonious energy, your home and work place should be organized and free of clutter. Physical dirt carries its own vibration, which may interfere with the energetic environment you want to create. Therefore, it is spiritually beneficial to regularly dust, vacuum and sweep. If you have wooden or tile floors, you may add a few drops of essential oils like Rosemary and Lavender to your cleaning products to clean on an spiritual level as well as a physical one.

As you clean, imagine the adverse energy dissipating. If you sweep with a broom, open the door and sweep the dirt out, visualizing all of the adverse energy going out with it. When you clean with your vacuum, visualize the energetic aspect of the dirt as you remove it from your home.

Traditionally, house washes like the following formula, which is brewed as a tea or decoction and strained, may be used as mop water for inside or outside the home or business. If it is strained through very fine filters, it may be placed into a spray bottle and sprayed around the house for protection. Take care not to over-saturate fabrics and carpeting and ventilate the area well until the moisture dries.

House Cleansing and Protection

1 gallon Water
1/2 cup Peppermint
1/4 cup Angelica root
1/4 cup Basil
1/4 cup Sage
1/4 cup Hyssop

Combine the above ingredients and bring them to a boil. Reduce the heat and allow this potion to simmer for several minutes. After it is cooled, strain it and use it to wash down the inside and outside of your home or business. Afterward, use a clean cloth to wipe down all of the surfaces inside your home or business to cleanse them of their old adversarial vibrations and bring new ones, which are harmonious with your purpose.

Living plants and flowers in your home or place of business help create a more harmonious environment. Grow herbs like Bay, Basil and Rosemary in your kitchen. Keep lucky plants like Bamboo and Malabar Chestnut, which is known as the "Money Tree" in Feng Shui, around your home or business.

Running water helps to purify your environment and exorcise negative energy. Install fountains and aquariums in areas where adversarial energy is persistent. Chimes and bells, also, spiritually cleanse and purify the environment around your home or business.

Regularly burning high quality incense or using a diffuser that disperses essential oils purifies and raises the spiritual vibration of a place. Diffusers filled with essential oils of Peppermint, Basil, Eucalyptus, Lavender and Rosemary serve a dual purpose of destroying bacteria and mold in the air at the same time.

Crystals may be charged and blessed for protection and placed around the inside and outside of your home. Blessed Sea Salt or Holy Water may be sprinkled inside and outside the home.

A common, effective way to clear a place of negative energy is to light a bundle of White Sage and allow the smoke to drift around the room. Afterward, follow a similar procedure with a braid of Sweetgrass to invite helpful spirits back.

It is not absolutely necessary to do any of these things, but it is something to consider, especially if your home or place of business has been the scene of arguing, violence or other unpleasantness that could leave a lingering energetic impression. It is more difficult to achieve positive results when a dark cloud seems to be hanging over a place.

How to Create an Altar or Work Space

Many spells in this book ask you to do work at an altar or work space. You do not have to have a fully equipped altar to cast spells successfully. But, it may be helpful to have some of the proper tools and equipment and a place to conduct your work. It is important to have a clean work space where you can do your spell and leave it undisturbed for as long as necessary.

People who live alone are at somewhat of an advantage when it comes to spell casting. Not only do they have more time to practice gathering and focusing energy and more room to do their spells without the interference of others, but they have the luxury of having work space that will remain undisturbed by others over the course of days that it may take to conduct a spell.

Couples and families often like to have a special room in their homes dedicated to ritual and spell work. Those with less room to spare set up an altar in an inconspicuous part of the house. The benefit of this is that the area, once spiritually cleansed, remains relatively clean because people are not walking through it.

The altar usually features blessed and consecrated items, such as:

Athame (double-edged knife used for ceremonial purposes)
Candles and candle holders
Cauldron
Censer or Thurible (incense burner)
Chalice
Crucible
Images and other symbolic representations of helpful spirits
Wands for different purposes such as ceremonial or for the direction of specific types of energy

Typically, the elements are represented in some way.

Earth: Salt and sometimes a pentacle, which is, also, used to represent the fifth element
Air: The wand and incense
Fire: The athame and flame of the candle
Water: A cauldron or goblet filled with water

These representative objects are sometimes employed to charge other objects. For example, objects are charged with each of the elements by sprinkling them with salt, passing them through incense, directing energy at them with the athame or sprinkling them with water.

The expectation is, also, set up by the spell caster that once in the designated room or at the altar, only certain things such as meditation, rituals, invocations and spell casting are going to take place. This is a good way to both psychologically and energetically reinforce your purpose

Casting a Circle

Casting a circle is optional for most spells, however, it is something people like to do, especially when they feel there are forces working against them or they simply need additional reinforcements.

Many Wiccans cast circles to draw upon the power of their gods and center themselves in an energy vortex, which is sometimes called a cone of power. The Hermetic Order of the Golden Dawn ritual is similar to that used by Wiccans, but slightly more complex. Other ceremonial magicians cast simple circles for both power and protection, from within which they safely and effectively communicate with spirits.

Similarly, the Obeah practitioners of Africa and the aboriginal magicians of Australia, also, cast protective circles to facilitate spirit communication. Casting a circle may, also, be helpful to you if you are having difficulty focusing or meditating.

There are many ways to cast a circle ranging from the very simple to the complex, but the Wiccan method is very popular.

A Wiccan Circle

This circle-casting ritual varies slightly from practitioner to practitioner and coven to coven. The following is a simplified version, which you can use to call the elements, to generate power and for protection from adversarial energy. Use it at your discretion to enhance your spell work.

You will need four candles. Ideally, they should be of four different colors: Red; black; white and blue, however, four white candles will do.

Most Wiccans open and close the circle facing north, but older variations on the ritual open and close facing east.

Draw a circle on the floor, mark it out with masking tape

or draw it using the point of an athame or wand and simply visualize it. Use a compass to find the four directions, then place a candle at each point. If you are using colored candles, place the black candle at the north, the red candle at the east, the white candle at the south and the blue candle at the west.

North and black represent the earth
East and red represent fire
South and white represent air
West and blue represent water

Stand facing north in a powerful stance with your feet a comfortable distance apart, raise your arms in the air, palms facing outward. If you have an athame, hold it in your right hand and say, "All hail the Guardians of the Watchtower of the North. I call upon you, the powers of earth, to guard and oversee this operation." Afterward, trace a pentacle in the air with your right index finger or with the athame.

Then, walk to the east and repeat this procedure, except you will say, "All hail the Guardians of the Watchtower of the East. I call upon you, the powers of fire, to guard and oversee this operation."

Then, walk to the south and repeat this procedure, except you will say, "All hail the Guardians of the Watchtower of the South. I call upon you, the powers of air, to guard and oversee this operation."

Then, walk to the west and repeat this procedure, except you will say, "All hail the Guardians of the Watchtower of the West. I call upon you, the powers of water, to guard and oversee this operation."

Return again to the north and trace the pentacle one last time before walking into the center of the circle.

To trace the invoking pentagram, begin at the bottom left hand point, move to the top point, down to the bottom right hand point, to the left-hand point, to the right-hand point, and back to the bottom left hand point.

Do not go outside the circle, but perform your spell within it. You should have all the things you need already there within the circle and ready to be used.

After you have completed this operation, close the circle by starting in the north, again. Then, walk in the opposite direction, thanking each power for its presence and bidding it to go in peace. Address each element as follows, "Spirits of the north, I thank you and I bid you go in peace," as you go around the circle.

Trace your banishing pentagram as follows: Begin at the top point and move down to the bottom left point to the right point, to the left point, to the bottom right point and back to the top point.

A Simple Circle

Circle-casting rituals all incorporate the concept of the four elements, which are the spiritual precursors to life on the physical plane, to protect and form a circle that represents the universe itself with you as the creative force within it. But, your circle does not have to be created through an elaborate ceremony to be effective.

If you feel you need the extra protection and power of a circle, simply draw a circle on the floor using chalk, tape, your ritual knife or simply your finger. Some old-fashioned conjurers made two concentric circles of a similar size and wrote the names of angels or the Tetragrammaton around the circle's edge.

For the circle to be effective, you must see it as a representative of the universe itself, with yourself in the center of it as its master. Gather power into the circle through the charging meditation of fire and water as previously instructed. Use this circle to become completely focused on your purpose or as a powerful place from which to plan or conduct your spells or communicate with spirits.

When you cast a circle for money or wealth, imagine a swirling mist of green following you as you conduct the procedure. Visualize yourself surrounded by riches, money and jewels. The circle can, also, be used to meditate on drawing money and wealth. Light a green or gold candle, dress it in Rue oil or a Money or Luck Drawing Oil and meditate on the fulfillment of your needs and desires.

7 UNCROSSING AND ROAD OPENER SPELLS

Uncrossing and Road Opener Spells are concepts that come from American Hoodoo. Similar terms that might apply are "spiritual cleansing" or "exorcism." Uncrossing revolves around removing energies attached to a person, including negative thoughts or emotions that may be blocking success. Road Opener Spells are used to remove roadblocks to success that may not be directly associated with the person, but are in their outer environment.

Either of these types of spells may be used in cases where nothing seems to work or positive results seem to be only temporary. If you work spells for money and wealth, but the effects are not what you had hoped for or if the effects are not long lasting, you may actually be in need of an Uncrossing or Road Opener Spell. Usually either of these is enough to pave the way for greater success with other spells for money and wealth.

Uncrossing Spells are used in cases where you feel there are energies attached to you that are working against you or that you may be mildly jinxed. Crossed people may experience setbacks and difficulties choosing the right path in life.

Road Opener Spells are used when you feel those

energies and blockages are not directly attached to you, but obstacles to success are in your path. Blocked people have difficulty carrying out their plans because of outside circumstances that seem to be beyond their control.

Uncrossing

At some time, most people experience some degree of being crossed because we all have a tendency to accumulate negative energy. For most people, the procedure for uncrossing is a simple one that may involve nothing more than taking a spiritually cleansing bath over the course of one evening.

There are fairly rare cases, depending on your cultural background or associates, in which a person is actually hexed by a witch. A hex is a more serious condition than being crossed. Although, it is relatively unusual, the following two cases are examples.

In one case, a pretty and successful young woman became the target of a small mob of jealous colleagues. They flattened all of the tires on her car, sent death threats and eventually forced her to break the lease on her condominium and flee in terror. Fortunately, her Mexican grandmother was a knowledgeable curandera. She made a trip from the U.S. to Mexico so that her grandmother could do the work of lifting the hex placed upon her. After she returned home, the problems ceased entirely.

Another disturbing case involves a young woman who had unwittingly become involved in a love triangle and had suffered miserably because of it. She was energetically drained and terrorized by a jealous witch who had hexed her over ten years ago. Unlucky things happened to her, in part because of her own distraction and fright. A spiritual cleansing of her home only temporarily solved the problem. She and her house both had to be exorcised before the problem was finally resolved.

In each of these cases, the person knew that they had been hexed by someone and they were even sure who it was. Black magicians sometimes place such hexes on people and only through the knowledge and application of the dark arts can they be successfully resolved. But, such cases are unusual and it is likely that you would know if you had become a victim.

Fortunately, the vast majority of people are simply a little bit energetically contaminated at times. This is not due to any fault of the person or their wrong thinking. Nor, is it the result of a curse or hex consciously placed by another person. More commonly, people simply accumulate energy that is not conducive to the attainment of their goals and this must be cleansed before real progress can be made.

There are various degrees of this kind of contamination and the degree to which you feel you have been affected by it will determine how much work you need to do to eliminate it.

If you feel that you are only a little crossed, perform the Uncrossing Spell below on just one night. Afterward, if you still feel in any way disturbed or have a sense of not being aligned with your purpose in life, then you may want to continue the spell over the course of seven nights.

Also, if you feel that you received a lot of negative messages from your family or others around you with regard to money and the health of your money consciousness has suffered because of it, then you may benefit from performing an Uncrossing Spell over the course of seven nights. Each night, after you have completed the spell, on separate slips of paper, write down the ideas about money you are holding onto, which you feel are holding you back. You may have to dig deeply into your own subconscious to find these thoughts and the emotions associated with them. After you have written them down, destroy each slip of paper by burning it in a fireplace or crucible. Bury the ashes at a crossroad or far away from your home or business.

Uncrossing Spell

An Uncrossing Spell is a mild form of exorcism and like some other spells, they may have to be performed more

than once to set a permanent energetic pattern. There can be layers to the negative energies, so it may take time and any number of workings before they are completely purged.

You will need the following:

White candle
Uncrossing Oil (formula below)
Uncrossing Bath (formula below)

Anoint the candle with Uncrossing Oil, using a motion away from you. As you work the oil into the wax, visualize all of the negative energy surrounding you and all of your unwanted subconscious programming about money going into the oil and permeating the candle.

Uncrossing Oil

1/2 cup Almond oil
7 drops Bay oil
7 drops Hyssop oil
7 drops Lavender oil
7 drops Rose oil
7 drops Verbena oil
7 drops Vetivert oil (or a root may be added to the master bottle)

Make this oil by adding the above drops of essential oil to the Almond oil. If you do not have the essential oils, but you have the dried herbs, you may make this formula by adding a handful of each of the herbs to a pint or so of oil and allowing it to remain in a warm place for a couple of weeks. Strain the liquid and place it in a dark bottle with a tight lid. Always store your potions in a cool, dark place.

After you have anointed the candle, take an Uncrossing Bath.

Uncrossing Bath

Make a traditional Uncrossing Bath by brewing a strong tea using a handful each of Bay leaves and Hyssop blossoms. You may, also, add Rose and Lavender blossoms for calming and increased protection. Sage and Lemon are other herbs commonly used in Uncrossing formulas. Add these herbs or essential oils to your Uncrossing Oil or bath formula at your discretion.

Allow the herbs to boil in a gallon of pure water for several minutes before removing the mixture from the heat. Allow it to cool and strain it before adding any essential oils.

Recite the following incantation over the brew before adding it to your bath water:

"Purge me with Hyssop, and I shall be clean; wash me, and I shall be whiter than snow."

Alternatively, you may, also add a few drops of Uncrossing Oil to plain liquid Castille soap like Dr. Bronner's to make an Uncrossing Bath.

You may use this simple Uncrossing Bath right before conducting any spell. Some practitioners, also, use a bath like this one after working malefic spells to rid themselves of any negative energy they may have acquired.

After you have completed your bath, light your two anointed candles and recite Psalm 51 in its entirety, as follows:

"Have mercy upon me, O God, according to thy loving kindness; according unto the multitude of thy tender mercies blot out my transgressions. Wash me thoroughly from mine iniquity, and cleanse me from my sin. For I acknowledge my transgressions; and my sin is ever before me. Against thee, thee only, have I sinned, and done this evil in thy sight; that thou mightest be justified when thou speakest, and be clear when thou judgest. Behold, I was shapen in iniquity; and in sin did my mother conceive me. Behold, thou desirest truth in the inward parts; and in the hidden part thou shalt make me to know wisdom. Purge me with hyssop, and I shall be clean; wash me, and I shall be whiter than snow. Make me to hear joy and gladness; that the bones which thou hast broken may rejoice. Hide thy face from my sins, and blot out all mine iniquities. Create in me a clean heart, O God; and renew a right spirit within me. Cast me not away from thy presence; and take not thy holy spirit from me. Restore unto me the joy of thy salvation; and uphold me with thy free spirit. Then will I teach transgressors thy ways; and sinners shall be converted unto thee. Deliver me from blood guiltiness, O God, thou God of my salvation; and my tongue shall sing aloud of thy righteousness.O Lord, open thou my lips; and my mouth shall shew forth thy praise. For thou desirest not sacrifice; else would I give it; thou delightest not in burnt offering. The sacrifices of God are a broken spirit; a broken and a contrite heart, O God, thou wilt not despise. Do good in thy good pleasure unto Zion; build thou the walls of Jerusalem. Then shalt thou be pleased with the sacrifices of righteousness, with burnt offering and whole burnt offering; then shall they offer bullocks upon thine altar."

If you are planning on conducting this ritual for more than one night, snuff out the candle after a couple of hours. Otherwise, simply allow the to candle burn out, secure in the knowledge that, as it does so, it destroys any negative energy that may have surrounded you.

Repeat this entire procedure before casting spells or whenever you feel out of sorts, stressed or anxious.

Road Opener Spell for Success

Open up the road to riches and success with this spell, which is best performed at the dark of the moon. The purpose of a Road Opener Spell is to open the way, spiritually and materially, for good things to flow into your life. This is a good spell to perform if you feel your efforts are being blocked by external circumstances.

You will need the following:

Photo of yourself
Yellow 7-day candle
Purple taper or pillar candle
Green taper or pillar candle
Orange taper or pillar candle
Road Opener Oil
Road Opener Powder
Wealthy Way Oil
Money Drawing Oil
Needle or thorn with which to make an inscription
Sea Salt
Pyrite
Moldavite or Topaz
2 Lodestones
Large unbreakable bowl
Red mojo bag

Poke three small holes into the wax of the glass-encased, yellow 7-day candle. Place a few drops each of Road Opener Oil, Fast Luck Oil and Wealthy Way Oil into the holes. You will find the formulas for these potions in *Chapter 4. Formulary of Oils, Incense, Powders and Washes*. Glue the photo onto the outside of the yellow 7-day candle.

On the purple candle inscribe the word, "Wealth," then

anoint it with Wealthy Way Oil.

On the green candle inscribe the word, "Money," then anoint it with Money Drawing Oil.

On the orange candle inscribe, "Open Road," then anoint it with Road Opener Oil.

When you are performing a spell to attract good things, always anoint the candles by rubbing the oil toward you as you visualize what you want coming to you.

Set these three inscribed candles into their holders in the shape of a triangle with the orange candle at the top. Place the yellow 7-day candle in the center of the triangle.

From the yellow candle, make three lines or trails of Salt extending out to each of the other three candles.

Dress the Lodestones with Money Drawing Oil and place them by the green candle.

Dress the Moldavite or Topaz with Road Opener Oil and place it near the orange candle.

Dress the Pyrite with Wealthy Way and place it near the purple candle.

Take a ritual bath using several drops of Road Opener Oil or a Road Opener Wash. Take a large bowl with you and dip it into the bath water nine times and pour it out into the tub while meditating on your desires. Finally, take a bowl of your bath water and dump it out at the nearest crossroad. Then, return home without turning around to look behind you.

After you return home, light the yellow candle and strike the table three times while shouting, "Open the road!" each time. As you do this, visualize the waves of energy you are creating going out, far beyond you into the environment.

Light the orange candle and say, "The road to riches is open to me and my world is filled with golden opportunities. Good fortune follows me and all my efforts bear good fruit."

Then, light the purple candle and say, "The road to a good life is open to me, I am surrounded by love and powerful friendships, I recognize the good opportunities that come my way and my life is filled with the best and the finest of all things."

Then, light the green candle and say, "The road to prosperity is open to me, my life is filled with money and abundance, I have meaningful work that pays me well and I always make fortunate financial transactions."

Repeat, "Opportunity, Money and Wealth! Open the road!" Say this until you feel a great energy rising within you. Passionately feel these words and allow their spirit to overtake you so that you can think of nothing else. Then say, "Amen!" or "So mote it be!"

After the candles have burned out, collect the Lodestones, Pyrite and Moldavite or Topaz and place them in a red mojo bag. Tie it, dress it with Road Opener Oil and carry it as a talisman. Once a month on a full moon, feed the Pyrite with a pinch of iron filings and dress the bag with Road Opener Oil to keep its power strong.

Properly dispose of the candles and other refuse from this spell by burying it at a nearby crossroad. Never allow yourself to be seen or leave a trace of your actions. Return home without looking over your shoulder.

Afterward, dust or anoint yourself, your clothing, your money and financial papers with Road Opener Powder or Road Opener Oil.

Three Coin Road Opener Meditation

This is a simple meditation you may perform at any time during a full moon. It requires a little Van Van Oil, which is used to open the road and speed the success of any endeavor.

Rub three silver coins with Van Van Oil and charge them with electromagnetic energy. Then, with the coins in your pocket go to a location at night where you can look up at the full moon without the obstruction of trees or buildings in your view. Touch the coins in your pocket while meditating on your goals. When you have finished, rub the coins and say, "As I will it, so mote it be."

Ganesha the Lord of Obstacles Road Opening Spell

Lord Ganesha, the Lord of Success and Destroyer of Obstacles, is the elephant-headed god of India who will help you attract opportunities and money, while removing both spiritual and physical obstacles in your life.

Lord Ganesha has counterparts in Santeria and Voodoo, which are Santo Niño de Atocha and Eleggua, respectively. So, you may substitute either of them for Lord Ganesha in this spell.

You will need the following:

An image of Lord Ganesha (this may be a statue or a printed image)
Fireplace, old coffee can or other container in which you can to safely burn paper
Piece of paper or parchment and a pen
Green, silver or gold candle
Good Luck or Prosperity Incense

On the day of waxing moon, light a candle and allow yourself to go into a relaxed, meditative state.

Pass the image of Lord Ganesha through the smoke of Good Luck or Prosperity Incense. Then, place it upon your altar or work space.

Write a letter to Lord Ganesha and tell him what you need. Take your time with this. When you have finished, address Lord Ganesha by saying, "O Lord Ganesha, please help me to break the obstacles in my path so that I may accomplish my goals."

Then, in your fireplace or fire-safe container, burn the letter. Gather the ashes and rub them on the image of Ganesha while repeating the obstacle destroying mantra, "Om Gam Ganapataye Namah," 108 times. It is pronounced like, "Aum Gam Gah-nah-pah-tah-yea Na-ma-hah." Recite it on one low note, singing each syllable one after the other evenly and rhythmically.

As you repeat this mantra visualize waves of energy going out away from your body, influencing the atmosphere around you. See it rippling away from you in a ring just as you would see if you cast a stone into the water. With each repetition you are creating another wave that is influencing the environment in your favor.

The mantra in this spell is extremely powerful and will almost instantly reduce your feelings of stress and tension. Use it any time you wish. It is an excellent meditation and may help you prepare to perform any spell or begin any new endeavor.

Other Spirits Who Open Roads

Along with Lord Ganesha, numerous other spirits may be called upon for the purpose of opening roads. Those spirits associated with the planet Saturn, the Underworld, the crossroad and keys are very powerful allies for those who wish to arrange worldly affairs in their favor.

The African Orishas Eleggua and Ogun; the Greek god Pluto and the goddess Hecate; the Catholic saints St. Anthony, St. Expedite, St. Peter, St. Philomena; the folk saints Santa Muerte (Holy Death) of Mexico and St. Simon of Guatemala may be called upon for a similar purpose.

These spirits and the methods of appealing to them for this and other purposes is described in *Chapter 13. Calling Upon Spirits, Saints, Gods and Goddesses.*

8 SPELLS FOR MONEY

Use these spells to banish debt and increase the flow of money into your bank account. Use the money to pay your bills and grow your savings.

Banish Debt Candle Spell

This debt banishing spell is best begun during the dark of the moon on a Saturday.

You will need the following:

Paper and pen
3 White or black candles
White Sage bundle or Sage oil
Green, silver or gold candle
Silver coin (preferably a Mercury Head dime)
Fireplace, large coffee tin or other safe place to burn a piece of paper
Money Drawing Oil
Green mojo bag

Make a list of all of your debts along with the name of the person or company to whom they are owed. Pass the paper and one of the white or black candles through the smoke of the White Sage bundle. Alternatively, anoint the edges of the paper and the candle with Sage oil using a motion away from you.

Dim the lights in the room. Then, light the white or black candle and meditate on the flame while you imagine your life without debt. When you feel you have given sufficient energy to these thoughts, take the paper with the debts written on it and burn it while calling upon Hecate, Hades, Pluto, the Norse Goddess of the Underworld Hel or any other Underworld spirit.

As you burn the paper, call upon the spirit by name, as follows: "N., I call upon your powers to destroy these debts, release their energy from my life and purify them in the earth. Let none be harmed as you bring this problem to a resolution. Bring me wisdom, inspiration and peace. By the power of three times three! So mote it be!"

Allow the candle to burn down completely. Repeat this procedure over the course of three nights. After the third night, bury the ashes and the refuse of the three candles off your property or throw it into running water.

On the following Friday or Sunday, preferably on the night of a waxing moon, anoint the green, silver or gold candle with Money Drawing Oil using a motion toward you. Light this candle. Afterward, hold the coin above the flame at a safe distance, but where you can see its light from the candle reflecting off of it. Then, place the coin on your altar with the head up.

Address the spirit you are working with, again, saying: "N., ruler over gold and silver, let this coin be a conduit for your wealth and abundance. Fill my life with all I need and more."

Meditate on your needs being fulfilled and being able to live the life you've always dreamed of in comfort and wealth until the candle burns out.

Bury the remains of the candle in your yard. Place the coin in a mojo bag and carry it with you. Once a month, on a full moon, anoint it with an oil formula for good luck, money or wealth.

Blessed Tip Jar

If you have a job where you rely on tips or sales commissions, this spell may help you increase your income. Begin the following ritual to create a Blessed Tip Jar on a Friday or Sunday night during a waxing moon.

You will need the following:

Glass jar with a lid (green glass is ideal)
Bayberry, dried
Lavender, dried
Orris root, dried
Sage, dried
2 Lodestones
Several coins
7 Green, yellow or white votive or tea light candles
Money Drawing Oil

Place a pinch each of Bayberry, Lavender, Orris root and Sage into the jar along with the coins. Anoint the two Lodestones with Money Drawing Oil. Place them in the jar and screw the lid down tightly.

Take this jar outside or to a window where you can hold it while looking up at the moon without being noticed or disturbed by anyone. Hold the jar between your palms and mentally charge it with the elements of fire and water. Then, fill the jar with your intention to increase other people's generosity toward you and to magnetize more tip money or increase your sales commissions.

Anoint the candle with Money Drawing Oil and place it in its holder. Place the candle on top of the jar or in front of it. Then, light it and speak the following incantation:

"Through the vivifying force of the elements,
By the magnetizing power of the moon,
Accomplish my will,
Multiply the flow of money to me,
By three times three,

As I say it, so shall it be!"

When the candle has burned out, place the jar in a window sill where the beams of the full moon can shine down on it and magnetize it. Bury the candle refuse in your garden or near your doorstep.

Every night for the next seven nights, anoint a few coins, especially those you've just earned as tips, and place them in the jar. Gently shake the jar and repeat the incantation. Leave the jar where it can be magnetized by moonbeams.

After the seven nights have passed, place the jar beneath your bed or in a drawer where it won't be disturbed or found by anyone else. Once per week on a Friday or Sunday, feed the jar by adding a few more anointed coins to it or sprinkling several drops of Money Drawing Oil into it to maintain its power.

Spell to Magnetize Money

The following money magnetizing spell is best performed during a waxing moon.

You will need the following:

Money Drawing Incense
Money Drawing Oil
White candle
Silver candle
Gold candle
Green or red mojo bag
6 to 8" piece of red yarn
2 Lodestones
Iron Filings

Anoint each candle with Money Drawing Oil, using a motion toward yourself.

Arrange the three candles in the shape of a triangle as follows: Place the white candle at the middle point closest to you. Place the gold candle to the left and the silver candle to the right. The candles should be set 6 to 9 inches apart.

Anoint the Lodestones with Money Drawing Oil and place them inside the mojo bag. Add a pinch of iron filings. Then, tie the bag with the red string.

Light a small amount of Money Drawing Incense upon your altar. Pass the mojo bag through the smoke of the incense. Then, place it in the middle of the triangle.

Light the candles and chant the following incantation while visualizing heaps of gold and silver coins all around you:

"Money, money come to me,
Gold and silver, three times three,
To meet my needs and help me fulfill my destiny,
comes wealth and abundance, three times three!
Let come no harm because of this charm.
So mote it be!"

Allow the candles to burn down. Then, collect the mojo bag with the Lodestones and keep it in your pocket or inside your clothes. Once per week on a Thursday or Sunday, feed the Lodestones inside the bag with a pinch of iron filings and a few drops of Money Drawing Oil while repeating the incantation.

Money Drawing Cake
(Spicy Cake with Cream Cheese Frosting)

Bake this spicy cake, which contains herbs to draw money and wealth, as an offering to your favorite god, saint or nature spirits. Serve a slice of cake to them and leave it overnight upon your altar or at the base of a tree with which you have a special spiritual rapport.

The best time to perform this spell is on a Sunday or Thursday during a waxing moon.

Ingredients:

2 tsp. Baking Powder
1/2 tsp. Baking Soda
2 1/2 cups White Flour
1/2 tsp. Allspice
1 tsp. Cinnamon
1/2 tsp. Cloves
1 tsp. Ginger
1 tsp. Nutmeg
1/2 tsp. Sea Salt
1 1/2 cups Dark Brown Sugar
4 Eggs
3/4 cup Salted Butter (softened)
1 cup Milk
1 tsp. White Vinegar
9 Coins, cleaned and wrapped in waxed paper or tin foil (optional)

Directions:

Place the baking soda and baking powder in a large mixing bowl.

Add the flour and say, "Holy Demeter, Goddess of Wheat, fertility and abundance bless this cake and all of those who partake of it."

Add the Allspice and say, "Spirit of Allspice, give us your blessings of good fortune."

Add the Cinnamon and say, "Spirit of Cinnamon, bless us with your power and expedite our good fortune."

Add the Cloves and say, "Spirit of Cloves, bless us with great wealth."

Add the Ginger and say, "Spirit of Ginger, bless us with heightened intuition and crown us with success."

Add the Nutmeg and say, "Spirit of Nutmeg, bless us with all the money we need."

Add the salt and say, "Creature of Earth, we ask for your protection and blessings."

Add the brown sugar and say, "Spirit of Sugar, sweeten and enrich our lives."

Stir these dried ingredients together.

Then, add the eggs. As you break each one, say, "Nourish us with your life force."

Add the softened butter and say, "Shower us with your golden blessings."

Add the milk and say, "Nourish and bless us with growth and abundance."

Finally, add the vinegar and stir the mixture thoroughly.

Preheat the oven to 350 degrees. Apply non-stick cooking spray to a 9" x 13" (33 x 23 cm) rectangular cake pan.

Pour the batter into the pan.

Some people like to bake actual coins into the money cake. This is optional and should, of course, be done very carefully. Soak the coins in lye soap water or in a little borax, then boil them in water to sanitize them. Afterward, wrap each one in tin foil or waxed paper. Place the wrapped coins on top of the batter. They will sink as the cake bakes.

Bake for 45 minutes to one hour. Allow your cake to cool on a wire rack.

Once it is completely cool, you may apply the frosting.

Cream Cheese Frosting Recipe

Ingredients:

1/2 cup Butter
8 oz. Cream Cheese
2 1/2 cups Powdered Sugar
1 tsp. Vanilla extract
Green food coloring (optional)

Directions:

Soften the butter and cream cheese to room temperature

and combine them into a medium-sized bowl. Blend until smooth.

Add the Vanilla extract and continue mixing. Slowly add the powdered sugar until you achieve the desired taste and texture.

To color the icing, place a small amount of it in a separate bowl. Add a few drops of green food coloring and mix it in thoroughly using the tip of a butter knife. Add this to the larger portion of icing and blend it together. Repeat this procedure until you achieve the desired shade of green.

When the cake is cool, apply the icing using a spatula or butter knife.

Old-fashioned Money Drawing Oil Lamp

Vintage kerosene lamps are an elegant and cost-effective alternative to candles and may be used on an altar in place of a candle or alone as a spell to draw money. The following spell to create a Money Drawing Oil Lamp is best begun on a Thursday or Sunday during a waxing moon.

You will need the following:

Old-fashioned kerosene or paraffin lamp
Vegetable-based lamp oil
2 Lodestones
Pyrite
3 Silver coins
Personal effects
Bay leaf
Money Drawing Oil

Begin with a clean lamp and an empty oil compartment. As you add your Lodestones, small piece of Pyrite, coins and personal effects, concentrate on the purpose of each one. If you require a specific amount of money by a certain date, write this information on a bay leaf and insert it in the bottom of the vessel. Add a few drops of Money Drawing Oil or a similar formula and then fill the rest of the chamber with a vegetable-based lamp oil, which is available at many department stores and online.

Charge the contents of the lamp and concentrate on your need. Place the lamp on your altar alone or before the image of spirits you work with and invoke their assistance.

Tips for using an old-fashioned oil lamp:

Roll the wick up and trim each of the corners slightly to keep the glass chimney from becoming blackened. Then, roll it down so that only 1/4 to 1/2" appears at the mouth of the burner. If you have just installed a new wick, wait a few hours before lighting it so it has time to soak up the oil.

After you light the wick, adjust the size of the flame by turning the knob on the side of the lamp. Then, place the chimney on top.

Always treat oil lamps with the same caution you would use with candles. Place them on a stable surface where they will not be disturbed and do not leave them unattended. Refill the reservoir with oil frequently. Do not allow the oil to burn away completely.

Hoodoo Money Drawing Oil Lamp

A very simple, beautiful style of natural oil lamp is commonly used in Hoodoo spells. Hoodoo oil lamps are powerful, economical substitutes for candles.

To draw money, create this elegant oil lamp on the night of a waxing moon.

You will need the following:

Orange, Grapefruit or Yam
Vegetable oil
3 Allspice berries
3 Cloves, whole
Black Obsidian, Pyrite or Green Aventurine
Personal effects
Money Drawing Oil
Wick
Wick tab

Halve an Orange or Grapefruit and carefully remove the fruit while leaving the peeling in tact. Alternatively, create a hollow in the center of a large Yam by scooping out the center portion. This will be the reservoir for your oil and other items.

Add the Allspice, Cloves, gemstones and personal effects. Pour oil into the reservoir. Cut a short piece of wick and place it in the center of a wick tab or a slice of cork, which has been pierced in the center. Place the wick and the tab on the surface of the oil where it should float. Then, light the wick.

Another variation on Hoodoo vegetable oil lamps can be made using a glass or a heavy Pyrex vessel. Do not use globular shaped vessels like wine glasses, however, because they can easily break if the flame floats under the edge if the glass. Place your herbs, stones, personal effects and drops of magical oil into the vessel. Add water up to approximately an inch from the top. Optionally, add a few drops of green or yellow food coloring. Pour a thick film of vegetable oil over the top of the water. Place a short piece of wick inserted through a wick tab on the surface. If the layer of oil on top of the water is thick enough, the wick and tab should float.

Always stabilize your Hoodoo oil lamps in a bed of sand or stones for fire safety.

Money Pot Spell

This Money Pot may be used alone or incorporated into other spells and rituals.

You will need the following:

Small cauldron or pot
3 Silver coins (Mercury head dimes are ideal)
2 Lodestones
Gold or Silver magnetic sand
Money Drawing Oil
Green or yellow candle
Piece of paper
Charms

Choose a cauldron or pot small enough to fit comfortably on your altar. Anoint the Lodestones with Money Drawing Oil or a similar formula. Place them in the pot and sprinkle magnetic sand on them. You may substitute iron filings for magnetic sand.

Add the charms, which may be four-leafed Clovers, coins you've found that were laying face up and other objects that represent money or good fortune to you.

Whenever you anoint items or place them into the pot, speak to them as if you were addressing an intelligent entity and instruct them as to how they are to help you. This can be specific and complex or as simple as saying, "Bring the money I need to me."

If you need a specific amount of money, write that amount and the date by which you need it on a slip of paper. Anoint the edges of the paper and the green or yellow candle with Money Drawing Oil. Place the paper under the Money Pot. Then light the candle and allow it to burn down as you concentrate on your needs.

Once per week, on a Thursday or Sunday, feed the Lodestones with a pinch of magnetic sand and sprinkle a few drops of Money Drawing Oil onto the items in the pot to maintain its power.

Maia Multiply Your Money Spell

This 7-day spell is intended to help you multiply your income. Maia is the Roman goddess of growth and increase and the mother of the fleet-footed god Mercury. The month of May is named after her and the first 15 days of this month are sacred to her.

This spell is best begun between the dates of May 1st and May 15th. But, it may, also, be begun during a waxing moon on a Thursday or Sunday.

You will need the following:

7 Silver coins (Mercury Head dimes are preferred)
1 T. Hawthorn blossoms
1 T. Cinnamon
Green mojo bag
Red ribbon or string

Place the coins into the bag. Sprinkle dried Hawthorn blossoms and powdered Cinnamon inside and tie the bag up with a red ribbon or string.

Hold this bag between your palms and charge it. Then, recite the following incantation:

"O Holy Maia Maiestas, Mother of Mercury,
Daughter of Fire and Earth,
By the power of the seven planets in heaven,
Multiply my money by seven times seven."

Carry this bag with you for seven days. Every morning spend a few minutes charging it and reciting the above incantation. After seven days, place it in a drawer or beneath your bed.

Ploutos Candle Spell for Money

Ploutos is the Greek god of money and wealth. He is the son of the agricultural goddess Demeter and a demigod. He is not to be confused with Pluto, the god of the Underworld, although, both are considered gods of riches. Ploutos was responsible for distributing riches to the deserving until he was blinded by Zeus. Afterward, he gave money and riches to all, without discrimination or consideration of their worthiness.

This money spell is especially useful for people who have a blockage with regard to feeling unworthy or undeserving. It is best when performed during the time of a waxing moon.

You will need the following:

Green pillar candle
Money Drawing Oil (or a similar oil formula)
Piece of paper

Make two notches equally distanced from each other on the side of the green pillar candle. Anoint it with Money Drawing Oil using a motion toward you. Place it in a sturdy holder. Write your petition or your wish on the paper and place it underneath the candle holder.

Then, relax and spend a couple of minutes charging the candle with the energy from your palms. Afterward, light it.

Infuse it with your intention by reciting the following incantation:

"Ploutos, god of riches and money,
Shower me with grains of gold,
Grant to me the riches and bounty,

Bring me a treasure of wealth untold."

Meditate on your specific wish for money until the candle burns down to the first notch. Then, snuff out the flame.

Repeat the procedure on the second night, allowing the candle to burn down to the next notch before snuffing it out.

On the third and final night, repeat this procedure, allowing the candle to burn down completely. Afterward, gather the remains from this spell and bury them in your yard.

Green Money Bottle Spell

Perform this spell during a waxing or full moon.

You will need the following:

Green glass bottle
7 Copper coins from your native land
7 Silver coins from your native land
7 Coins of any kind from other countries
7 Bay leaves
7 Cinnamon sticks
7 Cloves
7 Sesame seeds
7 Mint sprigs
7 Nutmegs
7 Grains of Rice

Place the above coins, herbs, seeds and grains into the bottle. Then, hold it in your hands and focus on charging it with energy.

Afterward, recite the following incantation:

"Spirits of the herbs and of copper and silver, do your duty! Increase my supply of money and bring prosperity to me."

Keep this bottle near wherever your store your purse, wallet or safe to attract a steady flow of money.

Spell to Get Money in an Emergency

Sometimes unexpected circumstances arise in which funds are needed in a hurry. This spell is for such occasions when you have an unanticipated bill to pay or some other urgent need for money.

You will need the following:

Rue 7-day candle (or a green or yellow pillar)
Red Fast Luck Oil
Money Drawing Oil
Piece of paper or a photocopy of a pertinent document
Fire safe container

Anoint the candle with Red Fast Luck Oil. If your candle is not the pullout variety, poke a little hole in the top layer of wax with a screw driver and pour a few drops of oil into the hole.

On a blank piece of paper, write the name of the person or company owed and the amount of money required. Alternatively, use a photocopy of a pertinent document, such as a bill or invoice. Anoint the edges of the paper with Money Drawing Oil and place it beneath the candle.

Then, light the candle and recite the following incantation:

"As this candle burns, universal forces are aligned in my favor,

To allow me to have the money I need to fulfill this obligation.

The money I need comes, yet no one will be harmed by this endeavor.

Free me and all my kin from this frustration and worry.

By the power of three times three! So mote it be!"

You may do this spell all at once, allowing the candle to burn down completely. Alternatively, if time permits, you may conduct the spell over the course of three or nine nights, snuffing the candle out after an hour or so each night. On the last night, allow the candle burn out completely. Burn the paper in a fire safe container. Then, collect the ashes and the candle refuse and bury it in your yard or near your home.

Money Drawing Poppet

Poppets or "voodoo dolls" are a fundamental part of Western European witchcraft in which a doll is used to represent a person. In this spell, the money drawing poppet represents you and the financial needs of your home or business.

Use the following procedure to make a Money Drawing Poppet to place on your altar, in your home or place of business.

You will need the following:

White or green candle
Money Drawing Incense
Money Drawing Oil
White Sage bundle
Paper and pen
Scissors
Green flannel, cotton or muslin
Needle
Green thread
Spanish Moss (available from craft stores)
Basil, dried
Chamomile, dried
Rosemary, dried
Quartz crystals
Any charms or buttons that represent money and good luck
to you

Purify your work area as well as the cloth, needle, thread and decorations you will be using to make the poppet by passing the smoke of a White Sage bundle around them.

Anoint the candle with Money Drawing Oil using a motion toward you. Then, light it. Anoint the crystals with Money Drawing Oil and set them aside.

Then, begin working on your poppet. Draw a figure in the shape of a gingerbread man. Stitch around the edges, leaving a relatively large opening at the head so you can get your fingers into it.

Once it is stitched, fill the body of it with Basil, Chamomile, Rosemary and the anointed stones. Then, stuff the head with Spanish Moss, allowing it stick out over the top to represent hair. Stitch this into place. Attach the charms and embellishments.

Then, light the Money Drawing Incense. Pass the poppet through the smoke and speak to it as you do so. Instruct it by saying, "I consecrate you by the powers of earth, air, fire and water. You are to bring money, prosperity, wealth and good luck to me and to this place. So mote it be!"

Then place the poppet where it won't be touched or disturbed by others. If this happens, it must be reconsecrated by passing it through incense and speaking to it, again.

Money Drawing Knot Spell

Obtain dark green yarn or embroidery floss. Pull strands of your own hair out of your hairbrush. Rub the hairs between your hands to create what looks like a thick fiber or cord. Braid this cord of your own hair into the green yarn or embroidery floss.

Tie nine knots in the braided strand while visualizing piles of money coming to you.

As you tie each one repeat the following incantation, then blow into the knot and cinch it tightly:

"God and Goddess, let money flow toward me in a way that harms none,

Let my needs be met with ease so I may fulfill my life's purpose.

[Insert your specific request.] So mote it be!"

Bury the braided and knotted cord nine inches deep in your yard.

Hindu Spell to Relieve Debt and Money Problems

Use this spell to relieve household debt and encourage the flow of money into your home.

You will need the following:

Flour
Water
Sugar
Pond with live fish

Create 108 pea-sized balls of flour and water. Then, take each of the balls in hand and repeat following mantra as you feed it to fish:

"Om Shreem Namah."

It is pronounced like: "Aum Shreem Nah-ma-ha."

At sunrise on the morning of the following day, each person in your household must bathe and then throw a handful of sugar out the door of your house as offering to the insects and other small creatures.

To Prosper and Make Good Decisions About Money

This spell to create an amulet should be performed on a Sunday at sunrise, during a waxing moon while facing eastward.

You will need the following:

Gold ring or pendant
White Sage bundle
Green or yellow candle
Money Drawing or Prosperity Oil

Choose a ring or pendant of, at least, 14 carat gold. You may choose something you already have in your possession or purchase a special money drawing amulet. It is all right if the item has a setting, especially if it is an Emerald or other gemstone associated with prosperity.

Cleanse the item by passing it through the smoke of White Sage. Alternatively, hold the item under running water while you visualize the energy attached to it draining away. Plug the sink so you don't lose the item if you lose your grip on it. You only need to do this visualization for about ten seconds.

Anoint the candle and place in on your altar.

Light it and sit or stand before it facing eastward with your hands clasped together in front of you and the golden item resting between your palms. If you still have a little oil on your hands from anointing the candle, this is good. Take a couple of deep breaths and gather your power within you so you can charge the ring or pendant. Take your time to create a ball of energy constructed of the elements as instructed in the chapter on charging.

When you feel you have sufficient energy, see it flowing throughout your body as if it is an empty vessel. Allow it to come out of your palms and permeate the atoms of the ring or pendant until you feel you have completely emptied this energy into it.

Then, impregnate the energy in the ring or pendant with your desire. The mental imagery and emotion you put into this operation is more important than the words you use.

When you feel you have done this sufficiently, finish this procedure by saying the following words as if you are addressing the ring, itself:

"Every step I take is always the right one
Every decision I make is always the right one.
Money comes to me, and money clings to me.
This is how it is now and forever more. So mote it be!"

Place the item on your altar in front of the candle and allow it to burn down completely. Afterward, place the amulet on your finger or on a chain around your neck. Then, bury the refuse from this spell near your doorstep or in the soil of a potted plant inside your home.

Spell to Inspire Generosity in Others

Use this spell to create a charm to inspire generosity in anyone who passes near it.

You will need the following:

Green candle
Skullcap
Generosity Oil
Green yarn or embroidery floss
Burn a green candle, collect the warm wax and form it into a ball. Make a hollow in the middle. Add a sprinkling of Skullcap and a few drops of Generosity Oil. Form the entire mixture into a ball.

Wrap the green yarn or floss around the ball of wax until it is completely covered. Tie the cord securely and hang the ball above the doorway to your home or business. Anyone who passes under it will become very generous with you.

Preserve the power of this charm by anointing it every Thursday with a few drops of Generosity Oil.

Money, Money, Money Spell

Use this spell to attract all the money you need and more. Perform this spell for seven days at sunrise, beginning on a Thursday during waxing or full moon.

You will need the following:

Green pillar candle
White pillar candle
Money Drawing or Prosperity Oil
Needle or thorn with which to make an inscription

Inscribe your name on each of the candles. Make six equidistant notches on each of the candles to mark the point at which you will snuff them out on each day, except the last when it you allow them to burn down completely.

Anoint each candle with Money Drawing or Prosperity Oil.

Place the candles on your altar or working space seven inches apart from each other. Then, recite the following incantation:

"Money, money, money come to me,
Money and prosperity, three times three.
Fill my bank account with all it can hold.
Bring me an abundance of silver and gold.
So mote it be!"

On the seventh day, gather the refuse of this spell, bury it in your yard seven inches deep and forget about it.

Money Tree Spell

Most of us grew up being told that money doesn't grow on trees. This spell works on two levels, both to dispel this subconscious negative programming about money and to bring prosperity into your life in a proactive way. This is not a spell that works overnight, but it is designed to bring a greater awareness of life's natural abundance to you and later to provide you with material for your other prosperity spells, depending on which species of tree you choose.

You may plant a tree outside or use a potted tree inside your home.

Perform this spell on a Thursday during a waxing or full moon. Alternatively, choose another propitious time that best suits your intention.

You will need the following:

Sapling
Coins
Shovel
Bucket of Water
Pot (if your tree is going to be indoors)

If you choose to plant a tree outside, select an Ash, Oak, Poplar, Pine or a fruit or nut-bearing tree. Plant it near a favorite window or a place in your yard where you will frequently see it or pass by it.

Another good choice of tree, especially for people who do not have a lot of room or who are apartment dwellers, is the Bay Laurel tree, which can be planted in a pot. The Malabar Chestnut, known as the "money tree," is another excellent choice for indoors in homes or offices.

If you are planting an indoor tree, put a small layer of dirt in the pot before transplanting it. If you are planting a tree outdoors, dig a hole sufficiently deep to plant your tree. Then, hold the coins in your left hand and speak to them, as follows: "Nourish this money tree that it may provide protection and prosperity to my family and me."

Place the coins into the hole or pot, plant the tree and cover it over with a sufficient amount of dirt.

Then, bless the tree and christen it in the name of an extremely wealthy person. As you water it say, "I bless you and name you, N., in the name of the Father, the Son and the Holy Ghost. Amen."

As you perform this entire operation, think of how this young sapling will grow into a mature tree that will bear fruit, nuts, leaves or bark. As you enjoy your tree, contemplate all of the ways it brings fruitfulness into your life.

If you choose a Bay Laurel tree, you can do a simple spell with the leaves from your money tree. Simply write a request for whatever you desire and burn the leaf to send the message into the ether.

White Flour, Candle and Coin Spell

Perform this spell when you want to keep a steady flow of money coming into your house and improve your finances.

You will need the following:

White Flour
3 Yellow candles
Money Drawing or Steady Work Oil
3 Silver coins
White or transparent plate
Mojo bag

Sprinkle a solid circle of flour around the outer edge of the plate. Anoint each candle with Money Drawing or Steady Work Oil. Inside the ring of flour, place the three candles around the plate at an equal distance apart. Rub the coins with Money Drawing or Steady Work Oil, then place them in the center of the plate.

Light the candles and let them burn down completely. Afterward, collect the three coins and place them into the mojo bag. Carry this bag with you.

Full Moon Prosperity Spell

Perform this spell for prosperity on the first night of a full moon, while facing northward.

You will need the following:

Silver plate or round tray
9 Silver coins
6 Green candles
Prosperity Oil
Silk handkerchief
Basil, dried

Anoint the candles with Prosperity Oil and arrange them in the middle of the plate in a circle so that they are approximately an inch apart from each other.

Pile nine silver coins in the center of the candle arrangement.

Light the candles beginning with the northern-most one. As you light each one, recite the following incantation:

"Light of growth and increase,
shower money and security on me.
Bring money, luck and prosperity.
So mote it be!"

Allow the candles to burn down, making sure that some of the wax drips onto the coins. Then, sprinkle the coins and wax with dried, powdered Basil.

Allow the coins to remain where the moonlight can hit them until the moon becomes completely full. Then, before the moon goes into its next phase, gather the coins, wrap them in silk and place them in a drawer.

If necessary, repeat the spell on the first day of the next full moon.

Fortuna Prosperity Spell

The Roman Goddess Fortuna is syncretic to the Greek Goddess Tyche. She carries a horn of plenty under one arm and an infant under the other. As you perform this spell, imagine her pouring out her good graces and abundance upon you, your house, your family or your business.

You will need the following:

Corn husk
Silver coin
Paper or parchment
Green yarn or ribbon
Good Luck Powder

"O, Great Goddess Fortuna, smile upon me.
Grant me abundance and prosperity
For all of the days of my life.
Thank you, Fortuna! So mote it be!"

Sign your name on the paper. Put the coin on top of it and sprinkle it with Good Luck Powder. Then, carefully fold it up, making each fold toward you, without spilling the powder.

Wrap the corn husk around the folded paper. Tie it all with a string and hang it over the entryway to your home or business to bring the blessings of good fortune, prosperity and abundance.

For a Prosperous House

To keep prosperity and wealth in your house and never want for anything, always keep the following seven items in jars where they are visible:

Brown Sugar
Cinnamon
Corn
Rice
Olive oil
Sea Salt
Wheat

Spell to Attract and Keep Money

Perform this spell over the course of three consecutive nights during a waxing moon to attract money and keep it from slipping through your fingers.

You will need the following:

1 1/2 to 2 gallons Water
White Carnation
Red Carnation
3 Cinnamon sticks
Bunch of Parsley
Bunch of Verbena
Bunch of Rosemary
Copper coin
Silver coin
Gold ring without stones
Castille or lye soap

Place all of the above ingredients, except the soap, into a pot and boil them for thirty minutes.

Remove this potion from the heat and let it cool. Strain

off the liquid. Don't lose the ring and coins!

Divide the liquid into three equal portions.

Over the course of three consecutive nights, take a bath with the soap and rinse yourself with a portion of this potion while repeating the following incantation three times: "Wealth and prosperity, come to me and dwell with me forever. Never depart."

Rose of Jericho Spell for Prosperity

The Rose of Jericho is a remarkable plant that folds itself up when it is allowed to dry, but opens up and appears to blossom when it is moistened, again. Use the transformational process of the Rose of Jericho to draw money and prosperity to your home or business.

You will need the following:

Small Buddha statue
7 yellow or green candles
5 Gold or Copper coins
Rose of Jericho, dried
Glass container
Water

Place a Rose of Jericho within a glass container. Arrange the statue and the coins around it. Then, fill the bowl with water.

Each day for the next seven days, light one of the candles. Hold your hands over the Rose of Jericho and charge it with energy. Speak to Buddha and ask him to bless your house with everything you need. Then, allow the candle to burn out.

9 SPELLS FOR JOBS AND EMPLOYMENT

Use these spells when you want to locate employment opportunities, gain influence over prospective employers, get the right job or change jobs. Use them to get your boss and co-workers to treat you right and to get a raise and all of the recognition you deserve.

Honest Employment

The power of reciting an incantation or prayer over Olive oil, then using it to anoint a person was familiar to the ancient Hebrews. This is a method of transferring the energy placed into the oil to a person. You may use this principle to find employment.

The Book of Psalms is a grimoire partially attributed to the sorcerer, King Solomon. Words of power for particular purposes were woven into the verses. To find honest employment, obtain a small glass bottle and fill it with Olive oil. Place a label on it that says, "Honest Employment."

Then, recite Psalm 111 over the bottle of oil with conviction, as follows:

"Praise ye the Lord. I will praise the Lord with my whole

heart, in the assembly of the upright, and in the congregation.

The works of the Lord are great, sought out of all them that have pleasure therein.

His work is honourable and glorious: and his righteousness endureth for ever.

He hath made his wonderful works to be remembered: the Lord is gracious and full of compassion.

He hath given meat unto them that fear him: he will ever be mindful of his covenant.

He hath showed his people the power of his works, that he may give them the heritage of the heathen.

The works of his hands are verity and judgment; all his commandments are sure.

They stand fast for ever and ever, and are done in truth and uprightness.

He sent redemption unto his people: he hath commanded his covenant for ever: holy and reverend is his name.

The fear of the Lord is the beginning of wisdom: a good understanding have all they that do his commandments: his praise endureth for ever."

Set this jar aside until you go to seek a job, then before you leave home, anoint yourself with this oil. You may, also, use it to anoint or feed your mojo bag or other job seeking talisman.

Ace the Interview

Get the edge on your competition by conducting this spell before a job interview. It is best performed on a Thursday or Sunday during a waxing moon. Although, it may be performed the night before an interview, it is better to do it several days ahead of time. This gives you time to relax and focus on your purpose and it gives the spell time to work.

You will need the following:

Yellow or white candle
Needle or thorn with which to make an inscription
Benzoin oil
Photograph of yourself
Deer's Tongue
Calamus root

Inscribe your name and your intention to ace interviews and get the right job on the side of the candle. Anoint it with Benzoin oil. Anoint the edges of the photo with a little Benzoin oil and place it on the altar next to the candle. Sprinkle a little powdered Deer's Tongue on top of and around the photo.

Then, use your index and middle fingers together to draw an invisible clockwise circle three times around the candle and photo. Sprinkle Calamus root over the invisible line of the circle you have just drawn.

As you do this, visualize yourself being asked questions and giving all the right answers. See the interviewer in your mind. Imagine that the two of you are on the same wavelength like old friends. Visualize yourself standing up at the end of your interview, thanking him or her and turning to leave, confident in the knowledge that you got the job. Allow the candle to burn down completely.

Mojo Bag to Get a Job

Create a customized talisman to get a job.

You will need the following:

Green mojo bag
Salep, High John the Conqueror root or an alligator's foot
Get a Job Oil
Nail clippings or a few strands of your hair
Gravel Root
Sea Salt
Cinnamon or Van Van Oil
Citrine or Cinnabar
3 Silver coins
Nephrite

Anoint a Salep root, High John the Conqueror root or a dried alligator's foot with Get a Job Oil.

Place this object into the mojo bag along with your personal effects and a few pinches each of Gravel Root and Sea Salt. Add a sprinkle of Cinnamon or Van Van Oil to the bag to speed its action.

Add a Citrine or a piece of Cinnabar and three silver coins to magnetize good luck, money and wealth. Add a piece of Nephrite to ease the transition into a new job.

Charge this talisman, as instructed in *Chapter 5. How to Charge Objects*. Once per week, anoint it with Get a Job Oil or bathe it in the smoke of Get a Job Incense and recharge it. You will have good luck and influence over employers and others who can help you secure employment when you carry this talisman in your pocket.

Job Changer Spell

Traditionally, frogs are a common feature of witchcraft. They are associated with the concept of death, rebirth and transformation. This is because they are creatures who live in two worlds, in the water and on dry land; they live in two different kinds of bodies, first as tadpoles and then as reptiles and throughout their lives, they shed their old skins for fresh, new ones.

They are not only capable of transforming and adapting themselves, but they are associated with changes in the climate such as clouds, rain and storms, which help to nourish and transform the earth. In fairy tales, frogs are creatures who have unexpected powers and abilities, which are revealed at the moment they are most needed.

If you would like to make changes in your work or career, such as getting into a different line of work or get a better-paying job with another company, then the spirit of the frog can help you. This spell is designed to help you make transitions of any kind. It helps you to prepare yourself for change and to send this request into the environment, where these vibrations can promote the changes you want to make.

You will need the following:

Effigy of a frog
Orange candle
Sage oil
Piece of paper

Orange is used in this spell because it is the color of dynamic growth in careers. It is symbolic of changing plans. If you feel more comfortable using green, yellow or white, feel free to make this substitution. Yellow promotes positive energy and helps us in matters where we require the approval of others to move forward. Green may be a better choice in cases where the desired change strongly involves the idea of making more money.

If you are artistic, make a little sculpture of a frog out of clay, wax or paper mache. Otherwise, find a statue of a frog, preferably one with an opening at its mouth. Whether you create the effigy of a frog or find one, your objective is to mentally and emotionally resonate with the spirit of the frog species. If you happen to live somewhere that has frogs as part of its natural surroundings, you may benefit from actually going outside and spiritually communing with them.

The main thing you must do to make this spell work is to find resonance with the transformational nature of these creatures. As you observe a real frog or hold the effigy of one in the palm of your hand, mentally project yourself into its body. Close your eyes for a few minutes and see yourself in the body of this creature. As you feel the ease of its ability to transition from dry land to water, see yourself with the natural ability to function well in a different career or work environment. As you see the frog shedding its old skin and emerging with a new one, imagine yourself with this natural transformative ability.

After you have completed this meditation and have begun to feel at one with the nature of this creature, anoint the candle with Sage oil, while meditating on the change you want to bring about in your life.

Light the candle. Then, write your specific request for a different job with more money or whatever you desire on a piece of paper and place it in the frog's mouth. If it is a ceramic frog with a hole in the bottom or if it is a planter with a hole, place your request there. If there is no opening, place the paper under the figure of the frog.

Continue to meditate on the changes you want to make in your life. Remember how it feels to be in the body and mind of the frog and how easy it is to transform while in this state. Then, focus your attention on the candle and mentally place your desires into it with all the emotional force you can muster. Once you have done this to your satisfaction, allow the candle to burn down completely.

The following morning take the candle refuse and bury it in your yard, near your doorstep or stick it into the dirt of a potted plant. Look for the opportunities to make the changes you desire, confident that you will make these changes easily and naturally because you now have the natural power to make this transformation within you.

Boss Tamer

This is a good spell to use before performing the Spell to Get a Raise or Promotion below or making any requests to an employer, including asking for a transfer, a raise or time off. It may, also, be applied to tyrannical bosses or unkind co-workers. It helps you to gain control over another person's mind and encourages him or her to behave more generously and kindly toward you.

You will need the following:

Small jar with a lid
White or light pink candle
Piece of paper
Cinnamon
Sweet syrup
Sugar

Write the person's name nine times in a column on the paper. Turn the paper 90 degrees and write your own name over the top of the first column nine times, crossing and covering it completely. Do this on a separate piece of paper for each person you wish to tame.

Place this paper in the jar. Add Cinnamon, syrup and sugar. Screw the lid down tightly. Light the candle on top of it and allow it to burn down.

Writing your name over the top of the person's name represents your domination of them. By placing it in the jar, you are applying sweetening vibrations to the person represented on the paper.

Spell to Get a Raise or Promotion

Perform this spell on a Sunday during a waxing moon before approaching your employer about a raise or promotion.

You will need three candles of different heights and colors, as follows:

Short: Green
Taller: Yellow
Tallest: Red

You will, also, need the following:

3 small pieces of paper
Needle or thorn with which to make an inscription
Uncooked Rice
Good Luck Oil
Get a Raise Oil
Bay oil

Inscribe your name on each candle along with the Old German rune Tiwaz, which looks like an arrow pointing upward.

Using a motion toward you, anoint the green candle with Good Luck Oil; anoint the yellow candle with Get a Raise Oil and anoint the red candle with Bay oil.

Write your name and your request on each of the pieces of paper giving the exact nature of your desire, including the title of the job you want, where you want to work and the amount of money you want to receive. Then, place one of the papers under each of the candle's holders, which you are to arrange as follows: The red candle on the far left, the yellow one in the center and the green one to the right.

Make a circle of rice around the candles.

Light each candle in turn. Each time, say aloud, "I only ask that you give me that which I deserve. Jupiter, reward me for my efforts."

Allow the candles to burn down completely.

Place some of the rice from this spell in your pocket when you go to ask for your raise or promotion.

Roll Out the Red Carpet Spell

Perform this spell to be treated like a V.I.P and to receive the accolades, rewards, admiration and recognition you deserve. The most propitious timing is during a waxing moon, on a Sunday morning at sunrise.

You will need the following:

Red ribbon, about a foot long at least an inch wide
Photograph of yourself
Hairs or other personal effects
White, purple or gold candle
Red Rose petals
Red Carpet Oil
Small box or bag

Stand facing eastward. Inscribe your name on the side of the candle and anoint it with Red Carpet Oil using a motion toward you. As you do this, imagine all of the honors, admiration and rewards that can be bestowed upon you by others coming to you.

Place the candle in its holder. Then, arrange the items on your altar with the red ribbon running toward you to represent a red carpet. Place the photograph of yourself in the center of the ribbon to represent yourself standing in the spotlight. Anoint a few of your hairs with Red Carpet Oil and arrange them on the ribbon a little above your photograph. Place the candle on top of the hairs and sprinkle the Rose petals in a circle around the photo and the candle.

Then, light the candle and say, "Be merciful unto me, for the sake of thy great, adorable and holy name, Chanan-jah, turn the heart of my prince to me, and grant that he may regard me with gracious eyes, and let me find favor and courtesy with him. Amen! Selah!"

Allow this candle to burn down completely in one day or snuff it out and repeat this operation over the course of seven days. You may, also, use a fresh candle each time you do the spell, anointing it and repeating the incantation as before.

Once you have completed this spell, gather the items and place them in a little box or tie them up in a cloth and put it where you won't find it or think about it, again, for a long time.

Spell to Get the Contract or Influence
an Employer to Hire You

This spell is for both independent contractors and those looking for steady employment.

You will need the following:

1 cup Chamomile blossoms
2 to 3 quarts Water
Large cast iron pot or cauldron

Learn the name of the person who is to make the final decision about hiring you or your company for a single job, an on-going contract or for an employment situation, which you hope will be permanent.

Place the blossoms and the water into a cast iron pot or cauldron and bring them to a boil. If you have a cauldron and can place it over an open flame for this operation, that's all the better.

As the water boils and steams, gather the electromagnetic energy within you and focus your attention on the boiling liquid, using the flow of energy from your finger tips or the force of your vision, charge it. Then, impregnate it with your intention to have your prospective client or employer hire you. Speak to the water with your mind or aloud. Always do whichever makes you most comfortable and doesn't cause a distraction.

Speak words of power, if you like. For example, speak the names of god in some language such as Yod He Vau He. Alternatively, make the sign of the cross, which activates the upper chakra centers and is a little like flipping a spiritual switch. You may, also, invoke the powers of potent gods, angels or other spirits like those listed in a later chapter.

Say something to the effect of: "N., you will hire me or my company for this job." Hold this idea and repeat it again and again, if necessary, to keep your focus on the water. Embellish it any way you like. For example, you might add wording to the effect that you or your company are ideal for the job and there is really no other viable option.

As the steam rises, it carries the impressions you have placed into the water out into the environment by means of the air. Visualize your prospective client or employer inhaling this air, which is impregnated with your desire. It goes into his or her body and becomes a part of them. If you perform this spell properly, they will hire you, believing that the idea was all their own.

End this operation before the pot of water evaporates. Do not leave a boiling pot unattended and take caution with the rising steam.

Spell to Get the Job You Want No. 1

If you know the name of your prospective employer, use this spell to gain control over him or her.

Small piece of paper
Bend Over Oil (formula below)

On a small piece of plain white paper, write the person's name nine times in a column. Then, turn the paper 90 degrees and write your own name over the top nine times. Anoint the paper with Bend Over Oil and place it into your right shoe before you go to a job interview.

Bend Over Oil

Almond oil
Allspice
Bergamot
Calamus root
Cinnamon
Frankincense
Honeysuckle blossoms
Licorice root
Vetivert
White Rose petals

Combine approximately equal parts of the above powdered herbs in a jar, cover it three times over with Almond oil. Keep it in a warm place for two weeks, shaking it once or twice per day. Afterward, strain and bottle it. For extra power, add a few drops of Van Van Oil.

Get the Job You Want Spell No. 2

If there is a particular job you want, but you don't know much about the person who does the hiring, use this spell.

You will need the following:

Green candle (a taper, pillar or pull-out)
1/4 cup Sage
3 T. Rosemary
9 Bay leaves
3 T. Gravel Root
1/4 to 1/2 cup Sea Salt
Piece of paper or classified ad clipping
Needle or thorn with which to make an inscription
Cauldron or metal coffee can in which to place burnt paper
Photograph of yourself, nail clippings, a drop of blood on a cotton ball or paper or a few hairs
Get a Job Oil or Job Hunting Oil
Mojo bag or other small bag or jar, in which to store herbs and salt from this spell

If you found the job you want in a newspaper, cut out the ad. If you found it online, print out the offer as it is written. If you heard about it by word of mouth, write down the name of the company, its location, the details about the department you want to work in, the position and the salary you want on a little piece of clean, white paper.

Combine the Sage, Rosemary, Bay leaves, Gravel Root and Sea Salt. Crush and pulverize them.

Inscribe your name and the exact purpose of your spell onto the candle. Express this in the present time and not as a future event. For example, "I, N., work at ABC Company as Loading Dock Supervisor."

Anoint the candle with Get a Job Oil or Job Hunting Oil, using a motion toward you while visualizing this job simply falling into your lap.

Place the personal effect on your altar. Put the candle in

its holder on top of or above it. Place the classified ad or piece of paper next to this. Sprinkle the herbs and salt in a circle around the candle, personal effect and paper.

Keep your cauldron or coffee can nearby.

Focus on charging the candle with electromagnetic energy. Do this until you sense it is full of this force.

Light the candle. Then, recite the following words: "I charge you to send this message to the world of spirits. Bring to me this job that I desire."

Allow the candle to burn down. Afterward, collect the herb and salt mixture and put it in a jar or bag. Bury the remains of the candle in your garden or near your steps. If this isn't possible, place it in a bag or box and put it in the back of a closet or drawer where it will be near you, but forgotten. Save the herbs and salt.

When you go for the job interview, place some of this herb and salt mixture you used in the spell in your pocket. Secretly, sprinkle a little on the floor of the prospective employer's office.

Alternatively, place it into a mojo bag. If you have a couple of small Lodestones or a High John the Conqueror root, anoint it with Get a Job or Job Hunting Oil and place it in the bag and take this with you to the interview to ensure success.

Steady Employment Spell

Use this spell if you fear losing your job or if you are a contract worker who fears that the supply of jobs might run dry.

You will need the following:

White pillar candle (or pull-out)
Needle or thorn with which to make an inscription
Steady Work Oil
Pinch of Gravel Root
Piece of paper

In a spiraling fashion, from top to bottom, inscribe the following on the candle: "+ [Your Name] + Steady Work." Repeat this inscription over and over until you reach the bottom of the candle.

Using a motion toward you, anoint the candle with Steady Work Oil.

On the piece of paper, write a description of the type of work you desire. Turn the paper at a 90 degree angle and write your name nine times over the top of this description. Draw "$" and "+" in each corner of the paper. Anoint the corners with Steady Work Oil. Sprinkle the center of the paper with a pinch of Gravel Root. Fold the paper toward you, to represent your desires coming to you.

Place the paper in front of the candle. Light the candle and meditate on your desire. Allow it to burn down or snuff it out and continue this meditation over several nights until it has burned down completely.

10 SPELLS FOR BUSINESS

Use these spells when you want to succeed in business, attract more customers, make more sales, obtain capital for your new business or expand a current enterprise.

Spell to Banish a Business Rival or Competitor

The most propitious time to conduct this spell to banish a business rival or competitor is on a Saturday during a waning or dark of the moon.

You will need the following:

Black candle
Black handkerchief or scarf
Photograph or other representation of the person or business
1 tsp. Lard
Clove oil
Dragon's Blood oil
Banishing Powder (formula below)
Red yarn or cord

Lay the handkerchief or scarf out flat on the altar. Place

the image or representation of your adversary in the center of it. Smear a little lard onto the photo and sprinkle Banishing Powder on top of it.

Banishing Powder

Combine and pulverize equal parts of the following:

Angelica root
Black Pepper
Cayenne Pepper
Clove
Garlic
Graveyard Dirt (obtained on a Saturday during a waning moon)
Nettles
Sea Salt

Inscribe your adversary's name or the name of his business on the candle. Then, anoint the candle with a few drops each of Clove and Dragon's Blood oil, using a motion away from you.

Envision your adversary and call to mind all of the things they have done to you to the point that you allow yourself to become enraged. Pour your rage into the candle as you rub it with the oil. When you feel that the candle is sufficiently filled with these vibrations, stop and hold the candle at arm's length as if it represents your enemy and you are showing him to an audience, as you say the following words:

"Here is N., right now he is very, very small and insignificant, but soon he will be even smaller. In a short time, he will wither and fade away to nothing."

Then, place the candle in a sturdy holder. Sprinkle a little more of the Banishing Powder around the entire ensemble, including the cloth with the item on it. Allow the candle to burn completely down until it finally expires in a puff of smoke and nothing is left but a little stump.

Wrap all of the refuse from this spell into the middle of the handkerchief, folding it in a motion away from you. Tie it securely with the red yarn or cord. As soon as you can, bury it near the person's residence, at a crossroad or in an old cemetery.

Fast Scrubbing Essence Wash

Use this classic Hoodoo wash formula to attract customers to your business. It is based on a 13-herb Fast Scrubbing Essence formula given by Zora Neale Hurston in *Mules and Men*.[3] Add it to your usual washing solution or use it alone to wipe down the floors, walls and sidewalks of your business to attract customers.

Ingredients:

Anise
Bergamot
Cinnamon
Dragon's Blood
Frankincense
Geranium
Hyssop
Lavender
Lemongrass
Myrrh
Orange blossoms
Rosemary
Wintergreen

There are two ways to create this wash. You may use 3 to 5 drops of each of the essential oils in a quart of pure water. Or, boil approximately 1/4 cup of each of the dried or fresh herbs in approximately a gallon of pure water. Make a strong decoction by simmering the brew for 10 minutes. Allow it to cool. Strain it and apply it with a mop or wash cloth.

Spell to Grow Your Business

If you want to increase your revenues and expand your business, perform the following spell on a Thursday night during a full moon.

You will need the following:

3 Silver coins
3 Bay leaves
Ink pen or fine-point marker
Bowl of Water
Mojo bag

Go to a place where you have a clear, unimpeded view of the moon. Meditate on your needs for several minutes. Consider three ways in which your business could be improved. Then, on the Bay leaves write a few words that embody each of these ideas.

Place the three leaves into the water. Then, place the three coins in the water one at a time.

Gently rotate the bowl in a clockwise direction three times. Then, leave it overnight in a safe place where the moonlight can shine down and magnetize it.

The next morning, remove the Bay leaves and the coins. Dry them and place them in a mojo bag. Cast the water into a pot of Ivy or into a patch of Spearmint, Peppermint or Lavender.

Carry the bag with you for nine days straight. Then, place it in a drawer where it won't be found.

Golem Sales Increaser

A golem is a simple being created by a magician to be a spiritual servant. Golem spirits are sometimes called familiars or servitors, although these terms can have subtly different meanings. The procedure to create a golem is similar to the one used to create a Money Drawing Poppet, but it is a more Hermetic one.

Before you begin creating a golem, spend a little time considering the exact purpose of your creature and an appropriate form and name for it based on its intended function. Its purpose should be singular and narrowly defined.

There is no rule to devising a name for a golem, except that it should be entirely unique and memorable to you. Ideally, it should represent an embodiment of the golem's purpose. It may be expressed in the form of an anagram. For example, if your golem's purpose is to make big sales, you might make an anagram of the words "big sales." In this instance, the being's name might become "Blissage." If you are familiar with foreign languages, you might do something similar in another language to create a name.

Decide on the form the being should take. If your business is stocks, then consider a bull. If you need to enhance selling power, consider a shark, since shrewd salesmen are referred to as sharks. If you want to bring customers to your store, consider making the golem in the form of a bird who brings worms to the nest or a bee who brings honey to the hive. Ideally, your being should be an entirely unique one and can be comprised of a combination of creatures that possess characteristics that suit your purpose.

A unique golem should be created for each separate purpose. For example, you may want one golem to increase sales for a specific product or service and another whose sole function is to find more buying customers for all that your business offers. It is, also, better if your assignment is a very specific one, such as, "Bring my total monthly sales to $10,000," rather than a general one, such as simply,

"Increase my sales."

You will need the following:

Air-drying clay
Black acrylic paint
Art paint brush
Simple Fluid Condenser (instructions below)
Small piece of parchment or plain paper
Small Emerald, Garnet, Citrine or other Quartz
Herbs (optional)

Cut a piece of parchment or plain white paper large enough to write a few sentences on. Soak the paper in the Simple Fluid Condenser formula given in *Chapter 13. Calling Upon Spirits, Saints, Gods and Goddesses*. You will need very little of this fluid for this purpose, only enough to soak the paper in.

To create Simple Fluid Condenser, brew a strong tea of Chamomile, Life Everlasting or Calendula blossoms. You may use a combination of these. Allow the herbs to boil for about 20 minutes, cool and strain the liquid. You will need less than a 1/4 cup for this purpose. Bottle it. Add 2 or 3 drops of your own blood to it and several drops of Vodka or other grain alcohol to act as a preservative.

Thoroughly moisten the paper with Simple Fluid Condenser, then allow it to dry completely. Afterward, write the words "Yod He Vau He" on the paper, followed by a statement of the golem's purpose and then the words "Shem ha-Mepharasch." The first phrase is the name of god or the Tetragrammaton, which is, also, a representation of the four elements and the creation of physical life. The last phrase is another name of god, which represents the 72 letters of his name, each representing an angel who had a role in creation.

This paper, along with a small piece of quartz, will be at the core of your creature. At your discretion, add a pinch of dried herbs, such as Bay leaf or Cinnamon, to enhance and direct the power of the golem.

Roll out a small piece of clay so that it is flat like a tortilla. Wrap the parchment around the crystal and place it in the center. Add the optional herbs. Then, fold the sides over to cover these items.

Add more clay to this core and begin to mold the shape of the creature around it. You do not need to be a talented artist. Your creature can take on any rudimentary shape. Or, it can be a more complex series of geometric shapes. For example, if you want to shape a crude bull, begin by forming a cone over the core. Then, as if you were building a snowman, place a ball of clay on top for a head. Then roll out two approximately equal pieces of clay and shape horns and attach them to the sides of its head. In the back, add a small tail in the same fashion.

Allow the figurine to dry completely before applying a coat of black paint to it.

You now have a body for the spirit of your golem. Charge it, as instructed in *Chapter 5. How to Charge Objects*.

Blow on the figure to breathe the spirit of life into it. Then, say, "I name thee, N."

Using your index finger or athame, trace the symbol of a hexagram or six-pointed star, sometimes called the "Star of David," in the air just above the golem's head. This symbol contains all four elements within it and imparts energy. It is made by drawing an equidistant triangle with a point up and then superimposing another triangle of the same proportions over the top of it with the point down.

Then, sprinkle water on it and say, "N., I baptize thee in the Name of the Father, the Son and the Holy Spirit."

The golem is sent out and called back by you mentally. When you want to speak to the being, take a few deep breaths and go into a trance state. The creature exists outside of time and space, so you can contact it from any distance and speak to its mind.

To dispatch it, tell the golem its specific purpose and assign a particular goal for it to accomplish. When it has carried out your orders, call it back into its body. To preserve its energy, wrap it in silk and place it where it will not be touched or discovered by anyone.

The being must be fed with your own energy, just as you charged it at the beginning of its life. It may be fed with your breath and a few drops of your blood. Usually once per week is sufficient, however, if you fail to feed it, it may begin to drain your energy or go out of control. If this happens, simply break the statue you created and hold its remains under running water to destroy it. Afterward, you can create another.

Some magicians like to assign an expiration date to the being. For example, if you create it on a certain date, decree that it shall expire in exactly six months, one year, etc.

These beings can be used for an unlimited number of purposes, for example, to help you find beneficial business relationships, to locate information or for virtually anything your require.

Keep in mind that while you may be working to earn money, there are those who may be working against you. In the present culture, we are conditioned to take responsibility for what befalls us and not blame others for our misfortunes. Yet, the fact is, there are others among us who are ruthless, who would benefit from the hard work of others, who are essentially parasites on the backs of those who labor and create. Acknowledging this and working to destroy these harmful influences may pave the way to success where you have failed in the past, especially when these failings have not been due to your own weakness or folly. A golem may be created, named and consecrated to the purpose of protecting your business or finances from those who would do you harm in this way.

If you make many golems, you will find it beneficial to make a note about each one in a journal giving a name, description, purpose and other information, including a time of expiration, if you assigned one. This information should remain entirely secret. Never share the names of your beings with anyone, especially another witch, because it is by their names that they are called and controlled.

Every witch finds his or her own unique process in

making and working with these beings. Very precise information about the creation of such beings is given by Franz Bardon in *Initiation Into Hermetics*.

Spell to Increase Sales

The following is an excellent, although simple spell for increasing sales. It must be done regularly for the best results because it is designed to incrementally increase sales upon each performance. It is best begun on a Wednesday during a waxing moon.

You will need the following:

Green pillar candle
Needle or thorn with which to make an inscription
List of the items you wish to sell
Sales Oil
Paper (optional)

Inscribe the names and details of items you most wish to sell onto the side of the candle. Optionally, if you have a very long list of items, write this information on a piece of paper and place it beneath the candle.

Using a motion toward you, anoint the candle with Sales Oil. Light it and allow it to burn down completely.

Once it has burned, rinse the candle holder and throw the water into a flower pot in which a healthy plant is growing.

Entrepreneur's Prayer to Influence Investors

If you are starting a new business or expanding an existing one and are in need of business capital, perform this spell on a Sunday morning at sunrise while facing eastward.

You will need the following:

White candle
Money Drawing or Success Oil

Anoint the candle with a Money Drawing or Success Oil using a motion toward you. Then, recite the 4th Psalm seven times, as follows:

"Hear me when I call, O God of my righteousness. Thou hast enlarged me when I was in distress; have mercy upon me, and hear my prayer. O ye sons of men, how long will ye turn my glory into shame? How long will ye love vanity, and seek after leasing? Selah."

"But know that the Lord hath set apart him that is godly for himself. The Lord will hear when I call unto him. Stand in awe, and sin not. Commune with your own heart upon your bed, and be still. Selah."

"Offer the sacrifices of righteousness, and put your trust in the Lord. There be many that say, Who will show us any good? Lord, lift thou up the light of thy countenance upon us. Thou hast put gladness in my heart, more than in the time that their corn and their wine increased. I will both lay me down in peace, and sleep; for thou, Lord, only makest me dwell in safety."

Before you must speak to investors or make a presentation, say:

"O God, let me find favor in the eyes of these investors to the glory of thy holy name. Amen. Selah!"

Before you send out proposals to prospective investors, sprinkle Money Drawing or Success Powder on the papers. Then recite your prayer.

To Repel Bad People and Attract Good Customers

Sometimes a business will go through a period of time where it attracts too many nuisances and not enough quality customers. Use the following spell to attract good customers to your business and repel anyone who would cause trouble.

You will need the following:

Basil
Large Citrine cluster, piece of Emerald or Jade
4 single-terminated Smoky Quartz crystals
4 double-terminated clear Quartz crystals

Single-terminated crystals are those that have a point at only one end. Double-terminated crystals terminate in a point at both ends.

The cluster or large gemstone serves as a centerpiece that represents the prosperity of your business. Double-terminated quartz crystals represent the energy of your customers flowing in and out of your business. The single-terminated smoky quartz crystals work to cleanse and redirect the negative energy and unpleasant visitors away from your business.

Sprinkle dried, powdered Basil around the entrance to your business. Then, construct the following arrangement of crystals near the entryway.

Place the large stone at the center of the layout. Then, place the double-terminate quartz crystals in an arrangement like the points on a compass: North; south; east and west. Then, equidistant between each of the clear crystals place the smoky quartz crystals with the point facing outward, away from the center crystal at the compass points: Northeast; southeast; southwest and northwest.

Charge the crystals with your intention to filter and direct the energy flow at your place of business to bring good customers to you and redirect bad people away from you.

Queen Bee Spell to Increase Awareness of Your Business

Artemis, the hunter goddess of ancient Greece is, also, a goddess of bees, which are ancient symbol of abundance, health and wealth. In ancient Greece, her priestesses were called "Melissai," which is Greek for "bees." Her status as a bee goddess is indicated by the bees on the dress of the statue of Artemis of Epheseus, although, she is actually one of many bee goddesses who can be traced back 6,000 years to Sumeria.

In European-American folklore, as documented by Vance Randolph and Harry Middleton Hyatt, bees are a link to the spirit world. Swarms of bees are spoken to in order to spread the word about something important, to communicate with the spirit world and to receive favors.

Among the bees, the Queen Bee is the ruler of the hive. She receives special benefits including the best of accommodations and the best food, brought to her upon the heads of her servants. She has greater power than her drones because she is able to sting multiple times without dying. To be the Queen Bee is to live a royal lifestyle.

This spell will transform you into a royal bee commander and facilitate your communication with the bees.

You will need the following:

Image of a bee
Beeswax candle or ordinary yellow candle
Amber, Lemon Balm, Lemongrass, Lemon or Orange oil
Lemon Balm tea
Raw Honey
Bread
Small plate
Bee Propolis (Royal Jelly) tincture or powder (optional)

The image of a bee may be a drawing, something you downloaded from the internet and printed out, a piece of jewelry in the shape of a bee or a knick-knack.

Anoint the candle with Amber, Lemon Balm, Lemongrass or similar citrus oil. You may, also, combine these oils. You will only need a total of 5 to 7 drops of oil to anoint a taper or other small candle.

If your bee image is a solid object, anoint it with a little oil. If you are using a paper image, anoint the edges of the image with the oil or pass it through an incense of one of these herbs. Then, say, "I consecrate you to my brothers and sisters, the bees."

Prepare your altar with the candle and the image. Place a small plate with a slice of bread drizzled with honey in front of the candle.

Brew yourself a cup of Lemon Balm tea and sweeten it with Honey. Add a little Lemon juice if it suits your taste.

The food of the Queen Bee is Bee Propolis or Royal Jelly, so to assist in your spiritual transformation, you may, optionally, take a few drops of a Bee Propolis tincture or mix a little powdered Bee Propolis into some Honey and place it on the piece of bread.

Light the candle and recite the following incantation aloud with conviction:

"Artemis, oh, Artemis!
Thou who art Queen of Bees,
And of all the wild spirits of the forest,
Lo! here I call to thee!
And with what power I have,
I conjure thee to grant to me the favor I implore!
As I drink this nectar, I am the Queen Bee."

Take a sip of the tea.

Address the image of the bee. As you do this, keep in mind that you are not speaking to an inanimate object, but the spirit of all bees.

Tell the bees your needs, as follows:

"I am the Queen Bee, your loving ruler. I command that you shall spread the word about my business and bring to me all of the good customers and allies I need to make my business thrive and grow. Fly upon the wind and use your special powers to communicate to the world of spirits and the world of the living. Spread the word and return the sweet nectar of success to me."

Address the bee spirits with sincerity. Include the name of your business or specific items that you want to sell in your request.

As a symbol of your relationship to her, eat part of the bread and honey, leaving the remaining part on the altar as an offering to the Queen Bee, whose power you now share.

Allow the candle to burn out completely or keep your altar intact and complete this spell over a period of days. Once completed, bury the refuse of this spell in your garden or near your home.

From this point forward, you have a relationship with bees. So, when you see bees in nature, address them just as if you were talking to people. You are speaking to the spirit of the bees when you do this. So, tell them that you are their ruler and give them a task to perform. Ask them to bring you money, good luck, opportunities, more customers, more sales or whatever you need.

When your request is fulfilled, anoint and light a beeswax candle, thank the bees for carrying out your wishes and ask for their continued allegiance.

Santa Muerte Spell to Improve Business

Santa Muerte or Holy Death is a very powerful, non-judgmental ally to those who devote themselves to her. She has the ability to help you with anything your require. You will learn more about her in Chapter 13. Calling Upon Spirits, Saints, Gods and Goddesses.

Perform this spell to ask Santa Muerte to help you improve business.

You will need the following:

Gold Santa Muerte statue or dark yellow Santa Muerte 7-day candle
Silver or gold coins
Golden altar cloth
Benzoin oil
Bottle or small jar with a lid
1 to 2 cups grain alcohol
Glass of Water
Golden yellow colored candle (only use this if you are not using a Santa Muerte 7-day candle)

Cover your altar with a golden cloth. Place the Santa Muerte statue or a 7-day Santa Muerte candle in the center. As a substitute for a statue, you may use a skull made of ceramic or other material. Place a glass of fresh water on the altar near her image.

Anoint the candle with Benzoin oil. Place the coins and alcohol into bottle and swirl them around nine times in a clockwise direction. Place the bottle with the coins in front of the image of Santa Muerte. If you are using a separate candle, place it in front of the bottle. Light the candle.

Then, recite the following prayer:

"O Most Holy Death, I ask that you enlighten this place with your holy presence and cloak me with the mantle of your protection. I ask that you destroy all evil and adversity. Destroy all of my enemies great and small. Relieve me of all envy, poverty and hate. Please, grant me all of the customers my business needs to thrive and grow and grant me the ability to serve their needs in return." Make the sign of the cross as you say, "In the name of the Father, the Son and the Holy Ghost. Amen."

Allow the candle to burn down. Then, every morning for nine days in a row, sprinkle a few drops of the liquid from the jar into the corners of your place of business while calling out to Santa Muerte to bring you customers and prosperity.

Successful Buying and Selling Spell

Whether you sell new items and need to locate the best distributors and the best deals or whether you trade cars, collectibles, books, or antiques for a living or just for extra money, if you earn money buying and selling goods, this spell is for you.

It is intended to provide you with safety in your travels and success in your attempts to locate items at a very modest price, so that you may benefit from this alone or by reselling the items at a profit. It is, also, helpful in searches for rare items, art, books and antiquities and obtaining such items at a low price. This spell is adapted from one mentioned in *The Gospel of Aradia* by Charles Leland.

"Apply this spell daily before going forth to procuring or obtaining any kind of bargains at shops, to picking up or discovering lost objects, or, in fact, to finds of any kind. If he incline to beauty in female form, he will meet with bonnes fortunes; if a man of business, bargains will be his. The botanist who repeats it before going into the fields will probably discover some new plant, and the astronomer by night be almost certain to run against a brand new planet, or at least an asteroid. It should be repeated before going to the races, to visit friends, places of amusement, to buy or sell, to make speeches, and specially before hunting or any nocturnal goings--forth, since Diana is the goddess of the chase and of night. But woe to him who does it for a jest!"[4]

You will need the following:

Silver or white candle
Luck Oil or Success Oil

Anoint the candle with three drops of oil using a motion toward you. Then, light it and pronounce the following incantation to Diana:

"'Tis Tuesday now, and at an early hour
I fain would turn good fortune to myself,
Firstly at home and then when I go forth,
And with the aid of beautiful Diana
I pray for luck ere I do leave this house!"

"First with three drops of oil I do remove
All evil influence, and I humbly pray,
O beautiful Diana, unto thee
That thou wilt take it all away from me,
And send it all to my worst enemy!"

"When the evil fortune
Is taken from me,
I'll cast it out to the middle of the street:
And if thou wilt grant me this favour,
O beautiful Diana,
Every bell in my house shall merrily ring!"

"Then well contented
I will go forth to roam,
Because I shall be sure that with thy aid
I shall discover ere I return that which I desire [name the specific object, if possible],
And at a moderate price."

This incantation is to ensure that you will find the person who owns the items you desire to obtain. The goddess will put in his mind the inspiration to know what you are looking for and move him in your favor so that he will want to help you.

The original incantation for this spell involves the use of Holy Oil for anointing. The first line of the second stanza reads, "First with three drops of oil I do remove." This is a reference to Blessed Holy Oil being used to anoint the witch. Its purpose is to remove all evil influences and impart good fortune.

Creativity Spell for Business

Whether you work in a creative field like advertising or marketing or need to come up with a new product or service idea or just a new way to make money, this creativity spell can help to inspire you. It is best performed on a Wednesday during a full moon.

You will need the following:

Image of a spider
Cobweb
Yellow or purple candle
Creativity Oil (formula below)

Choose a candle color that best suits your purpose. Yellow is for lower intuition, such as feelings and hunches. Purple is for higher intuition, such as communication with spirits and connection to the akashic aspect of the ether where information can be obtained. You may use either or both of these colored candles, as you desire.

Anoint the candle with a few drops of Creativity Oil using a motion toward you.

Creativity Oil
To promote creativity in the arts and business

1 cup Almond oil
2 T. Angelica
1 T. Eyebright
1 T. Rosemary
1 T. Wisteria
Several drops of Sandalwood oil

Combine dried and powdered herbs into the oil and allow them to macerate for, at least, two weeks. Strain the liquid. Add Sandalwood oil. Store the potion in a dark bottle.

As you prepare this potion, call upon the nine gods or goddesses, Athena, Anatum, Maya, Danu, Sarasvati, Oshun, Brighid, Apollo and Thoth, all of whom are associated with creativity and inspiration, to further empower it.

Then, obtain an image of a spider such as an image from a book, a drawing or a little sculpture and some cobweb from around your home. Place the cobweb in a little glass container or a plastic bag.

Place the spider upon your altar in front of the candle. Light the candle. Then, speak to the spirit of the spider, addressing her as Arachne, who is a great weaver among the ancient Greeks. Ask for her wisdom in weaving your strategy. Ask her to attract creative ideas and catch them in the web you have collected.

After you have completed this spell, take a bath with several drops of Creativity Oil added to the water. As you relax, the solution you seek may come to you before your bath water has cooled.

Place the spider and the web in the same container and put it near your bed for creativity inspiring dreams. Anytime you need inspiration, light a candle to Arachne and make your request. Then, take a relaxing bath with the Creativity Oil.

11 SPELLS FOR LUCK AND GAMBLING

Use these spells when engaging in games of chance, whether your game is the lottery, races, sporting events, sweepstakes, casino games or playing the stock market. Use them to improve your luck and to get an edge by sharpening your mental powers.

Historically, spells to manipulate luck are a common aspect of witchcraft. They often involve the creation of a charm or talisman, which you wear or touch when you gamble or place in your wallet or your home. Sometimes spirits are invoked to arrange the outside environment in a way that tilts the wheel of fortune in your favor.

Holy Water sprinkled around the inside and outside of your home repels bad luck. Growing Sunflowers in your garden or burying Dandelion roots at the four corners of your property draws good luck to your home.

High John the Conqueror roots, rabbit's feet, alligator's feet, two-tailed lizards, spiders, four-leafed Clovers and other herbs, bones and things in nature are carried for good luck. Ancient talismans based on descriptions from old grimoires are carried for the same purpose. They are blessed, anointed and treated as if they have a spirit of their own. Carrying such an object with you, especially allowing it to touch your skin bonds you to the amulet and it to you, as it begins to pick up your personal energy frequency.

Four-leafed Clovers

The four-leafed Clover is an old charm to ward off evil and attract good luck. The association of four-leafed Clovers with good luck is well known and was documented in Adams County, Illinois in the 1930s by the folklorist Harry Middleton Hyatt.

"The person who finds and picks a four-leafed clover will have good luck."

"Let the finder of a four-leafed clover put it in a Bible and good luck will come to him."

"When you have found a four-leafed clover, stick it into your shoe and you will be lucky as long as the clover leaf remains there."

"To obtain good luck after you have picked a four-leafed clover, you must wear it in your left shoe."

"If a four-leafed clover is found on the 1st of May, keep it and you can secure whatever you desire."

"Finding a four-leafed clover is a sign that you will inherit money."

Hyatt's research indicates that five-leafed and six-leafed Clovers are generally regarded as bad luck. These should not be plucked, but if you do pick one by mistake, giving it away will transfer the bad luck to an enemy.[5]

Spell to Create a Luck Ball

There are many different methods of creating a Luck Ball, also, called a "jack ball," which may be designed for a variety of purposes. Luck Balls are similar to mojo bags, but they have properties more in common with golems, in that each ball contains a spirit of its own that is related to the witch who created it or the person for whom it was created.

The procedure for creating this particular Luck Ball is derived from the book, *Old Rabbit the Voodoo, and other Sorcerers,* by Mary Alicia Owen who documented the folk practices of Voodoo practitioners of African and American Indian descent living along the banks of the Missouri River in 19th century St. Joseph, Missouri.[6] The original spell was performed on behalf of Charles Godfrey Leland by a man she called the King of Voodoo

You will need the following:

4 lengths of white yarn, each 48" long
4 lengths of white sewing silk, each 48" long
Another long length of white yarn with which to wrap the ball
2 body hairs from the owner of the Luck Ball (Red Clover may be substituted)
A pinch of Grave Yard Dirt (from the grave of a criminal)
Tin Foil (Not Aluminum; available at craft stores)
Whiskey
Piece of silk fabric
Red flannel mojo bag
Hemp or flax thread

Fold each strand of yarn in half and then in half, again. Place them neatly on a table in front of you a couple of inches apart from each other.

Fold each strand of sewing silk in half and then in half, again. Place one of these on top of each one of the skeins of yarn.

Pick up the first of the combined skeins and, treating them as if they were one cord, form the first of four equidistant knots beginning at one end.

Once you have tied the knot, take a small sip of whiskey and repeat the following incantation four times:

"God before me, god behind me. God be with me.
May this ball fetch all good luck to me.
May it tie down all devils.
May it bind down my enemies before me.
May it bring them under my feet.
May it bring me increase and plenty.

May it bring me faithful friends.
May it bind them to me.
May it bring me honor.
May it bring me riches.
May it bring me my heart's desire.
May it bring me success in everything I undertake.
May it bring me happiness.
I ask for it in the name of god."

After you have recited this for the fourth time, spit on the knot. Then, form the second knot in the combined skein, repeating this procedure of sipping whiskey, reciting the incantation and spitting on the knot. Do this until you have made four such knots in each of the four skeins.

When you have completed this, wad the four skeins up to form a little nest. Place a small piece of the foil, the hairs and Graveyard Dirt in the center of it. Wrap a layer of tin foil around this. Then, take a length of white yarn and wrap the ball, just as you would to create a ball of yarn for knitting. Make the ball about 1 to 1 1/2 inches in diameter and leave a tail anywhere from 8 to 10 inches long. This ball may, also, be used as a pendulum, so leave it long enough to be comfortable for you to use this way.

Wrap the completed ball in a layer of tin and place this in a piece of silk. Keep it in a red flannel mojo bag. Wrap the neck of the bag with hemp or flax, but do not knot it. Tying it will tie up the flow of energy.

This bag is to be kept near you at all times. When you need extra luck, remove the ball from the bag, hold it and allow it to touch your skin. Traditionally, the bag is worn pinned inside your clothing with the string slung over your left shoulder and under your right, so that the ball rests under your right armpit.

Every week the Luck Ball must be given the Eau de Vie or water of life, which is whiskey. Sprinkle a few drops on the ball and speak to it to remind it of its purpose to bring you good luck in all endeavors and protect you from all adversity.

According to the King of Voodoo, the devil is afraid of "four times four," which is why the theme of fours is used in this spell. It is important to understand that the term "devil" in traditional witchcraft does not usually have the same meaning that it does in Christianity. Instead, it is a reference to adversarial forces that, in this case, might stand in your way of good fortune.

The knots in the yarn represent your devils being tied down. The knots in the silk cloth represent your friends being tied to you and held beneath your feet, so they are in your service and look up to you.

Tin is a noble metal and it represents the brightness of the spirit in the ball. When Red Clover is substituted for hair, it represents the owner of the ball. Although, two hairs are preferable to use because they carry the personal vibration of the owner. Graveyard Dirt is used to blind the eyes of your enemy.

The layering of organic substances and metals in this talisman works to increase its power. This layering is very similar to the alternating organic and metal materials formula used by William Reich in his orgone energy accumulators.

The Horse Shoe for Protection and Good Luck

The arched shape of the horse shoe is a symbol found among the earliest relics in the history of mankind. Among the Caledonians, the earliest race of people in Scotland, it is associated with an ancient serpent king, the Nagendra whose worship originated in Ceylon. The horse shoe's shape resembles the first quarter of the moon, which is associated with Diana and her aspects as Hecate and Our Lady or Mary. In Egypt the symbol of a crescent moon was placed upon the most powerful gods and wearing one was a symbol of devotion to them.

According to Robert Lawrence in *The Magic of the Horse-shoe with other Folk-lore Notes*, the horse shoe is only one of many crescent moon shaped amulets. The beneficial nature of this shape relates to the timing of the waxing moon. "The growing horned moon was thought to exert a mysterious beneficent influence not only over many of the operations of agriculture, but over the affairs of every-day life as well. Hence doubtless arose the belief in the value of crescent-shaped and cornute objects as amulets and charms; of these the horse-shoe is the one most commonly available, and therefore the one most generally used."[7]

Old horse shoes were made of iron, which is associated with the planet Mars and the manufacture of weapons, as well as the life force and the blood, which naturally contains iron. Iron is used in both protective and malefic witchcraft to drive away evil forces or enemies. Old cemeteries are surrounded by iron fences to contain vampires, ghosts and other spirits from the grave. Iron is used in protective Witch's Bottles, such as the old Bellarmine bottles found buried under hearths throughout England and New England. It was once customary to bury iron knives beneath the threshold of a home to ward off evil.

Throughout Western Europe, horse shoes have been found nailed to Christian churches to repel the devil. *The Horse Shoe: The True Legend of St. Dunstan and the Devil; Showing how the Horse-shoe Came to be a Charm Against Witchcraft*, is a fanciful 19th century story about how a popular 10th century English saint got the best of the devil and made a deal with him that he would never enter any premises where the horse shoe is displayed. St. Dunstan was a blacksmith who nailed a horse shoe to the devil's foot and forced him to sign a contract in order to secure his release from this painful circumstance.

"...The Devil sendeth greeting: Know ye that for himself and heirs said Devil covenants and declares, that never at morn or evening prayers at chapel church or meeting, never where concords of sweet sound sacred or social flow around or harmony is woo'd, nor where the Horse-Shoe meets his sight on land or sea, by day or night, on lowly sill or lofty pinnacle, on bowsprit, helm, mast, boom or binnacle, said Devil will intrude."[8]

According to legend, a horse shoe promotes good fortune and bars evil, however, it is not credited with expelling it, so the horse shoe should be fastened above your doorway after you have cleansed and blessed the premises. The luckiest horse shoes are old, discarded or lost ones you have found.

To use the horse shoe as a protection from bad luck, place it over the door with the arch upward and the points down. When it is placed with the points downward like an archway, it closely resembles symbolism seen in Assyrian and Egyptian sculptures, signifying the mystical door of life.

To use the horse shoe for good luck, fasten a used iron horse shoe above the entryway to your home or business with the ends up, like horns or the crescent moon. Some people believe this position keeps the luck from running out.

Always hold a horse shoe in place with three iron nails.

Key Amulet for Good Luck

Keys, especially old ones, are amulets for good luck and to open the doors of success. Hecate, Ogun and St. Peter are all associated with keys. Tie two or more keys with a red ribbon and carry them as an amulet or hang them in your home or business for good luck.

It is especially lucky to find a key. When you find one, recite the following incantation:

"'Tis not a key which I have found,
Nor one which I shall bear around,
But fortune which I trust will be,
Ever my friend and near to me."[9]

Blowing or whistling into a key calls the assistance of good fairies who will help you in all of your endeavors.

Rue Luck Spells

Rue is commonly used in spells from a wide variety of sources. It is hung in doorways to guard against the entry of evil spirits and burned to dispel bad spirits from a place. It is used to send away bad luck and attract good luck; and to enhance mental processes and sharpen intuition. It brings strength and resolve and helps to heal from trauma.

Rue is used to bring heightened creativity and to improve vision both physically and spiritually. It was used as an antidote to poison and as an amulet against witchcraft by the ancient Greeks. It protects from accidents and energetic drain. It may be used to protect from a variety of different kinds of psychic and spiritual attacks.

There are many ways to use Rue to attract luck, money, success and other benefits into your life.

Keep a live Rue plant in your home for good luck and prosperity. To have good luck, take a little spring of it with you when you leave the house.

If you have had troublesome or quarreling people in your home, make a wash or burn an incense of Rue, Agrimony and a few drops of Van Van Oil. Then, recite Psalm 37 to completely clear the air of adversarial vibrations.

Begin your spell work with a cleansing bath using several drops each of Rue oil and Hyssop oil along with a cup of Sea Salt. This will purify your energetic field and help you to enter a calm, meditative state.

Warning: Some people are allergic to Rue and cannot allow it to come into contact with their skin. Rue contains tannins and is both a poison and an abortificant, if taken in very large doses. It should not be consumed, especially by those who are pregnant.

Rue Candle and Talisman Spell

To draw the protective and good luck drawing powers of Rue into your life, begin this spell on the night of a waxing moon.

You will need the following:

Green or white Rue (Ruda) 7-day candle or pillar candle
Hair or nail clippings
Rue oil
1/8 to 1/4 cup Rue, dried
Citrine
Silver coin
Mojo bag

Anoint the candle with Rue oil. If you are using a 7-day candle, poke a few holes in the top layer of wax and pour several drops of Rue into them. Otherwise, anoint the candle with several drops of Rue in a motion toward you while visualizing its positive influences coming toward you.

Light the candle. Then, in a sturdy thurible, set alight a small amount of dried Rue as a loose incense. Speak to the spirits of the Rue plant, "Spirits of Rue, protect me from all evil, bring me good fortune and all of the things I desire."

Then, meditate on the benefits of Rue and see the protection, good luck and other positive things you desire coming to you. Do this for several minutes, then allow the candle to burn for an hour or so before snuffing it out. Repeat this procedure for nine consecutive evenings.

On the ninth night, when the ritual is finished, collect some of the burnt Rue and place it into a mojo bag along with several of your own nail clippings or a few strands of hair, a Citrine and an old silver coin. Carry this with you for nine days. When you go to bed, slip the bag under your pillow. After nine days have passed, place it in the bottom of a drawer and forget about it. The positive vibrations from this spell will remain with you.

Spell to Create a Customized Rue Talisman

Use this spell to create a customized talisman to attract good fortune.

You will need the following:

White candle
Green candle
Needle or thorn with which to make an inscription
1' long piece of twine or yarn
Hyssop oil
Rue oil
Sea Salt
Spearmint, Peppermint or Wintergreen oil
Silver coin
Bayberry
Myrrh resin
Pine needles
Rue, dried
Citrine, Cinnabar, Bloodstone or other gemstone
High John the Conqueror, Orris or other root
Key, Lodestone or small medal (optional)
Mojo bag

After you have taken a purifying bath of Rue, Hyssop and Salt, inscribe your name on each of the candles. On the green candle, also, inscribe such words as "prosperity," "wealth," "success," "riches" and "good luck."

Anoint the white candle with a few drops each of Rue and Hyssop oil using a motion away from you. Place it on the left side of your altar.

Anoint the green candle with a few drops each of Rue and a Mint oil using a motion toward you. Place it on the right side of your altar.

Light the white candle first while saying:

"Forces of light and purity, cloak me in your protection in the name of the Archangel Michael. Amen!"

When this candle has completely burned out, light the green one while saying:

"Spirits of Rue, give me strength and vitality; give me inspiration and success; protect me from all adversity and bring me my heart's desire in the name of Barakiel the Angel of Good Fortune. Amen!"

While this candle burns, prepare your talisman by placing a small amount of Rue, Bayberry, Pine Needles and Myrrh into a Mojo bag. These herbs bring protection, money, wealth and enhanced intuition.

Include, at least, one stone and one root.

Include stones in accordance with your needs. For example, add Citrine or Cinnabar to attract money and customers; Bloodstone if you must travel for your work; Ruby if you must make important financial decisions or Tiger's Eye or Moonstone for enhanced intuition and inspiration.

Include a root for more power. High John the Conquer is used to dominate people and situations and win at games of chance; Salep (Lucky Hand root) for gambling, safe travel and luck finding employment; Orris root to attract the affection of others and for added protection and Ginseng for longevity and wealth.

Add other small items, such as medals or charms according to your purpose. For example, include an owl charm for wisdom; an old key to unlock doors of opportunity; a Tonka Bean for courage and good luck in business or a Lodestone to draw to you all that you desire.

When you have assembled your bag, set alight a small amount of Rue, Bayberry, Pine needles and Myrrh resin as a loose incense in a thurible and consecrate your talisman by passing it through the smoke. Charge your talisman, as previously discussed. Then, sew the bag shut or tie it with twine or yarn.

Carry this bag with you, in your pocket or around your neck. Pass the bag through any incense smoke or anoint the contents with a few drops of Rue oil about once per week to keep it energetically charged.

Rue, Vervain and Holy Stone Talisman

The following is a very old spell and incantation to consecrate a charm to the goddess Diana.

You will need the following:

Stone with a natural hole, which you have found
Vervain
Rue
Mojo bag

Stones that have natural holes in them have long been regarded as symbols of good luck, fertility, abundance and prosperity. When you find a stone with a hole in it, make a talisman by placing the stone in a bag with a little Vervain and Rue.

Then, recite the following incantation over the stone and the herbs:

"I have found a holy-stone upon the ground.
O Fate! I thank thee for the happy find,
Also the spirit who upon this road
Hath given it to me;
And may it prove to be for my true good
And my good fortune!"

"I rise in the morning by the earliest dawn,
And I go forth to walk through (pleasant) vales,
All in the mountains or the meadows fair,
Seeking for luck while onward still I roam,
Seeking for Rue and Vervain scented sweet,
Because they bring good fortune unto all.
I keep them safely guarded in my bosom,
That none may know it - 'tis a secret thing,
And sacred too, and thus I speak the spell:

"O Vervain! ever be a benefit,
And may thy blessing be upon the witch
Or on the fairy who did give thee to me!"

"It was Diana who did come to me,
All in the night in a dream, and said to me:
"'If thou would'st keep all evil folk afar,
Then ever keep the Vervain and the Rue
Safely beside thee!'"
"Great Diana! thou who art the queen of heaven and of
earth,
And of the infernal lands--yea, thou who art
Protectress of all men unfortunate,
Of thieves and murderers, and of women too
Who lead an evil life, and yet hast known
That their nature was not evil, thou, Diana,
Hast still conferred on them some joy in life."
"Or I may truly at another time
So conjure thee that thou shalt have no peace
Or happiness, for thou shalt ever be
In suffering until thou grantest that
Which I require in strictest faith from thee!"[10]

Carry this amulet with you for good fortune in all
matters.

The Conjuration of the Round Stone

Use this spell to create a round stone charm consecrated
to the goddess Diana. If you find a round stone, keep it in
your pocket as an amulet so that you will have good luck
with money and if you lend money, the debt shall always
be repaid to you. Never give it away or your luck will be
transferred and misfortune will befall you.

To create this charm, look toward heaven and throw the
stone in the air three times, catching it each time.

Then, recite the following conjuration:

"Spirit of good omen,

Who art come to aid me,
Believe I had great need of thee.
Spirit of the Red Goblin,
Since thou hast come to aid me in my need,
I pray of thee do not abandon me:
I beg of thee to enter now this stone,
That in my pocket I may carry thee,
And so when anything is needed by me,
I can call unto thee: be what it may,
Do not abandon me by night or day."

"Should I lend money unto any man
Who will not pay when due, I pray of thee,
Thou the Red Goblin, make him pay his debt!
And if he will not and is obstinate,
Go at him with thy cry of 'Brié - brié!'
And if he sleeps, awake him with a twitch,
And pull the covering off and frighten him!
And follow him about where'er he goes."

"So teach him with thy ceaseless Brié - brié!
That he who obligation e'er forgets
Shall be in trouble till he pays his debts.
And so my debtor on the following day
Shall either bring the money which he owes,
Or send it promptly: so I pray of thee,
O my Red Goblin, come unto my aid!
Or should I quarrel with her whom I love,
Then, spirit of good luck, I pray thee go
To her while sleeping--pull her by the hair,
And bear her through the night unto my bed!
And in the morning, when all spirits go
To their repose, do thou, ere thou return'st
Into thy stone, carry her home again,
And leave her there asleep. Therefore, O Sprite!
I beg thee in this pebble make thy home!
Obey in every way all I command.
So in my pocket thou shalt ever be,
And thou and I will ne'er part company!" [11]

Black Cat Bad Luck Reversal Spell

Use this spell to reverse bad luck and bring good fortune. Black cats are associated with both good luck and bad. While it is good luck to have a black cat in your home, it is considered bad luck if a strange black cat crosses your path from right to left. If he crosses from left to right, however, you will be assured of good luck and any adversity will become a thing of the past.

To conduct this spell, you will need the following:

Black cat figure candle
Black Cat Oil
Solomon's Seal or Myrrh

If you cannot obtain a cat figure candle, then a black pillar will do. Special reversal candles that are half black and half green are sold by some metaphysical shops for reversal spells like this one.

Anoint the candle with Black Cat Oil using a motion away from you. As you do this, imagine that all bad luck and negativity is leaving your mind and body and absorbing into the candle.

Burn a small amount of dried Solomon's Seal root or Myrrh as an incense and hold the candle in the smoke of it.

Speak as if you addressing the candle and say:

"I command you to absorb and destroy all bad luck and negativity from me on every level of my being. All bad luck you will now absorb and destroy. Every negative thought, every negative emotion, every negative thing that was ever said to me, you will now absorb and destroy."

If you are using a black cat figurine, turn the cat's body to the right to symbolize the cat crossing from left to right. Then light the candle and allow it to burn down completely. If there is anything left of the candle when the spell is complete, put the remains in a container and at the next opportunity bury the refuse off your property or at a crossroad.

Reverse Bad Luck Bath and Meditation Spell

Use this simple bath spell to release negativity and bring good luck.

You will need the following:

White candle
2 cups Sea Salt
Reverse Bad Luck Wash
Good Luck Oil

Draw a comfortable bath with the Reverse Bad Luck Wash and Sea Salt.

Light a white candle and meditate on the Salt drawing all of the negativity out of your body and into the water.

When you finish your bath, remain in the tub while you drain the bath. Close your eyes and see all of the bad luck and negativity going down the drain and out to sea to be forever neutralized as you say, "Bad luck is washed away from me, it flows down the drain and out to sea."

Gently dry yourself off. Then, anoint your body with any Good Luck Oil, starting with the bottom of your feet and working your way upward.

Reverse Bad Luck Recitation

If you have been working very hard, but your efforts are not producing the results you desire, before sunrise on three consecutive days, recite Psalm 4, as follows:

"Hear me when I call, O God of my righteousness: Thou hast enlarged me when I was in distress; have mercy upon me, and hear my prayer. O ye sons of men, how long will ye turn my glory into shame? How long will ye love vanity, and seek after leasing? Selah. But know that the Lord hath set apart him that is godly for himself: the Lord will hear when I call unto him. Stand in awe, and sin not: commune with your own heart upon your bed, and be still. Selah. Offer the sacrifices of righteousness, and put your trust in the Lord. There be many that say, Who will show us any good? Lord, lift thou up the light of thy countenance upon us. Thou hast put gladness in my heart, more than in the time that their corn and their wine increased. I will both lay me down in peace, and sleep: for thou, Lord, only makest me dwell in safety."

Afterward, on each of the three days, also, recite the following prayer:

"May it please thee, O Jiheje, to prosper my ways, steps and doings. Grant that my desire may be amply fulfilled and let my wishes be satisfied even this day, for the sake of thy great, mighty and praiseworthy name Amen! Selah!"

The holy name is called Jiheje. It is pronounced like "Ee-hay-yah" and it means, "He who is and will be."

If you wish to accomplish an undertaking by or through another person, proceed in all things as already stated above, with this exception. You must change the prayer as follows: "Let me find, grace, favor and mercy in the eyes of [Name], son (or daughter) of [Name], so that he may grant my petition."[12]

If you are employed and want to receive a pay raise, say the above prayer before the sun rises on seven consecutive mornings, before approaching your employer with your request.

Chinese Wash

Use the following house wash to exorcise bad luck and draw good luck to a home or business:

1 quart Water
13 Broomcorn straws
6 oz. liquid Castille soap
3 oz. Van Van Oil

Boil the Broomcorn straws in water. Allow this to cool. Remove the Broomcorn straws. Then, add the remaining ingredients. Use this potion to wash down the inside and outside of any building to dispel bad luck and draw good fortune to that place.

Good Luck Sprinkling Powder

Use this sprinkling powder to reverse bad luck, to attract money and to purify your home, yourself or your place of business.

You will need the following:

1/4 cup Galangal (Low John root)
1/4 cup Patchouli
1/2 tsp. Nasturtium seeds
7 drops Citronella oil
Holy Water
Copper coin

Combine dried Galangal, Patchouli and Nasturtium seeds in a mortar and pestle or a coffee grinder and crush them into a very fine powder. Add Citronella oil and a sprinkling of Holy Water. Store this mixture in a cool, dark place with a new copper penny in the jar.

There are many ways to use this powder. You may take some in the palm of your hand, go outside and blow it into the air while saying a prayer for what you desire. It may be included in sachets, mojo bags and used to dust yourself, your clothes and your sheets. And, it may be sprinkled around your home or office to bring good luck and prosperity.

Spells for Gambling

While luck spells are used in all kinds of circumstances to attract good luck and ward off bad luck, they are especially popular among gamblers. Spells for gambling essentially take three different approaches: Employing charms and talismans for good luck, as previously discussed in this chapter; divining the winning results in advance and influencing the outcome of events.

A common feature of gambling whether it is card games or bingo is the lucky charm. Bingo players are especially well known for sitting at long rows of tables with their bingo cards, surrounded by an arrangement of troll dolls, rabbit's feet and similar talismans.

In American Hoodoo, High John the Conquer root is the main gambling charm. But, to understand the true significance of High John it is important to understand its historical meaning and the origin of its powers.

High John the Conqueror Gambling Charm

According to the folklorist and Hoodoo practitioner Zora Neale Hurston, "High John the Conqueror" refers to an African Prince who was brought to America. She wrote extensively of his adventures in her book, *The Sanctified Church*, in which he is portrayed as a shaman, a clever trixter and a champion of freedom.

In *Mules and Men*, she explains that the name "John" is, also, represented in American folk heroes like John Henry, the larger than life African-American steel-driver swinging his hammer to build the railroad tracks. In Western European tradition, particularly among the Old Germans, the hammer represents power and justice. It represents a law greater than that of man and in this American folk tradition it is the power to overcome tyranny and oppression and to ultimately dominate the devils of adversity and those who would seek to dominate and enslave us.

High John the Conqueror represents domination in all matters. It has within it the fiery forces of the planet Mars and the spirit of the machete-wielding African Orisha Ogun. Therefore, it is one of the most powerful ingredients in charms and potions in American Hoodoo. It is this representation of self-mastery and victory over all tyrants that must be remembered when we think of High John the Conqueror.

So, while High John the Conqueror is the gambler's charm, it represents far more than just that. The root contains the fiery spirit of John, himself, and all he represents. According to Hurston, after his death the spirit of this prince went back to reside in Africa, but he waits to be called upon by his people whenever he is needed.

To use High John the Conqueror as a gambling charm, obtain a whole root. Never use one that has been sliced or crushed. Anoint it with whiskey, Gambling Oil or traditional Hoodoo formulas like Has No Hanna, Three Jacks and a King or Jockey Club, which are given below. Keep this talisman in your mojo bag or in your pocket and touch it before participating in any game of chance.

Has No Hanna
(Hoodoo gambling and good luck)

1 cup Almond oil
1/4 cup Night Jasmine blossoms

This old, original Hoodoo formula has been the subject of some controversy. In *Mules and Men,* Zora Neale

Hurston indicates that Has No Hanna is Jasmine, however, it appears that it is not the common species, but a Night Blooming Jasmine of the botanical name Cestrum Nocturnum.[13] It is native to the West Indies and South Asia and is commonly called Hasna Hena.

Three Jacks and a King Oil

This is another Hoodoo formula for fast luck and gambling success. Use it to anoint any gambling charm or talisman.

1/2 cup Almond oil
5 drops Cinnamon oil
5 drops Carnation oil
5 drops Wisteria oil
5 drops Orange oil

Jockey Club Oil
(French Formula)

1/2 cup Almond oil
16 drops Rose oil
16 drops Tuberose oil
5 drops Cassia oil
5 drops Jasmine oil
3 drops Amber or Ambrette oil

The original formula called for Civet cat oil.[14] The African cat from which this oil is obtained is endangered. Therefore, Amber or Ambrette oil is substituted here.

To make Jockey Club Cologne, omit the Almond oil base. Instead, combine the other ingredients in this potion to a base of 7 parts distilled water and 3 parts Everclear grain alcohol or Vodka.

Add a few drops of Geranium oil to this formula to impart courage, confidence and protection.

Anointing Oil for Protection, Good Luck and Gambling

Use this anointing oil for protection, good luck and to win at games of chance.

You will need the following:

Small glass bottle
Olive oil
Label

Obtain a small glass bottle, fill it with Olive oil and place a label on it that says, "Good Luck and Protection." Then, recite Psalm 23 in its entirety over the bottle, as follows:

"The Lord is my shepherd; I shall not want. He maketh me to lie down in green pastures: he leadeth me beside the still waters. He restoreth my soul: he leadeth me in the paths of righteousness for his name's sake. Yea, though I walk through the valley of the shadow of death, I will fear no evil: for thou art with me; thy rod and thy staff they comfort me. Thou preparest a table before me in the presence of mine enemies: thou anointest my head with oil; my cup runneth over. Surely goodness and mercy shall follow me all the days of my life: and I will dwell in the house of the Lord for ever."

Set the jar aside until you are ready to gamble. Then, anoint yourself with this oil, which you have consecrated.

Precognition Spells

Precognition or knowing the outcome of an event before it occurs is another way to win at gambling. It takes a little practice to develop your natural precognitive ability. The following spells will help you get started.

Spell for Prophetic Dreams

This spell to produce prophetic dreams is best begun during a waxing moon on a Monday or Thursday night about an hour or so before your scheduled bed time.

You will need the following:

Dark purple fluorite or clear quartz crystal ball or skull
Dream Powder (formula below)
Sachet bag
2 cups Sea Salt
Lucky Dream Oil (formula below)
Silver or white candle
Piece of paper

It is ideal to have a small crystal ball or crystal skull for this operation, although any shape of crystal will do. Dark purple fluorite is ideal, but a clear crystal will do fine, also. Cleanse the crystal by placing it in a window sill where it can be purified by the sun's rays for an hour or so.

Place a little Dream Powder in a sachet and put this under your pillow.

Dream Powder

2 parts Basil
2 parts Mugwort
2 parts Lavender
1 part Silver magnetic sand

Afterward, take a ritual bath with several drops of Lucky Dream Oil and Sea Salt.

Lucky Dream Oil

1/2 cup Hemp oil
7 drops Calendula oil
7 drops Frankincense oil
7 drops Heliotrope oil
7 drops Mimosa oil
7 drops Jasmine oil
7 drops Sandalwood oil

After you have completed your bath, write the name of the event you want to know the outcome of on a piece of paper. If you have a ticket or card for the event, such as a lottery ticket, place this on the paper.

Anoint the candle with a few drops of Lucky Dream Oil.

Place the paper on your altar and put the candle in its holder on top of it. Then, light the candle.

Attain a meditative state. Then, place your palms a few inches away from the base of the candle on each side and charge it. Direct the energy you have put into the candle by imposing your will on it. Mentally or aloud, say to the candle, "Bring the power to dream the future to me. Let me see the future of this event tonight in my dreams."

After you feel you have sufficiently filled the candle with your intention, hold your crystal and go into a deeper meditative state. Allow yourself to become completely relaxed. When you have accomplished this, hold the crystal ball between your palms, charge it and speak to it in a similar way.

Allow the candle to burn down a little before you snuff it out. Perform this spell over a period of, at least, three nights, although you will achieve far better results if you do it every night for a longer period of time. As you continue to perform this spell regularly, your dreams will become more vivid and begin providing you with more specific information.

Place the crystal under your bed or hold it while you fall asleep. Envision a dark purple ball of energy filling your body as you drift off to sleep and reinforce your desire to dream about this particular future event.

Eating dark blue or purple berries or drinking juices of Acai berry, Blackberry or Blueberry right before retiring may help induce vivid dreams. Drinking Ginger and Lemongrass tea, also helps the body to create the chemistry needed to produce psychic dreams.

It is important for you to be able to remember your dreams upon awakening. There are two ways to encourage this ability. Firstly, before you go to sleep at night, say to yourself, "I will dream the numbers for the lottery (or the outcome of a race, etc.) and I will recall it very easily upon awakening." Secondly, when you awaken, do it very slowly. If you are not the kind of person who leaps out of bed at the instant the alarm rings, you will have an easier time remembering your dreams. Upon awakening, allow yourself to languish in the twilight state for a few minutes. Try to recollect your dreams, just as if you were trying to access any other memory you possess.

Write your dreams down in a note book. Having this reference, along with the date of the dream will be very helpful to you when your prophetic dreams become stronger and more frequent.

You may dream certain numbers, be shown the outcome of a game or you may dream in symbols. Your dream journal will be especially important in understanding the symbolism of your dreams. There are very old dream divination books devoted to this subject, which can give you an idea of how this works. Examples of dream dictionaries are Madame Juno's *The Gypsy Queen Dream Book And Fortune Teller,* published by Obscure Press; *Aunt Sally's Policy Players' Dream Book* or *The Three Witches or Combination Dream Dictionary*, published by Lama Temple.

If you do not find these books of practical value as they are, they may help you develop your own strategy for understanding the numeric symbolism of your dreams.

Spell to Enhance Psychic Abilities

Perform this simple candle spell to open up your third eye. It is best begun on a Thursday during a waxing moon.

You will need the following:

Purple or dark blue candle
Psychic Oil (formula below)

Anoint the candle with Psychic Oil. Optionally, anoint your third eye center, which is in the middle of your forehead above your nose.

Psychic Oil

1/4 cup Almond oil
7 drops Frankincense
7 drops Marigold
8 drops Mugwort
7 drops Sandalwood
8 drops Thyme

Before lighting the candle, hold it between your palms for a few minutes. Relax and charge the candle. Then, speak to it in a commanding tone, as follows: "By the power of Jupiter, bring psychic powers to me."

Place the candle on your altar and light it. Spend some time meditating on receiving greater psychic abilities. After a few minutes, shift your consciousness to your third eye and focus on increasing the size of this energy center. Will it to open up, turn faster and become larger.

Do this for ten minutes or as long as you feel comfortable. Do not over tax yourself. Snuff the candle out and repeat this procedure over the course of several nights or until the candle has burned down.

Psychic development is discussed at greater length in the book, *How to Develop Advanced Psychic Abilities: Obtain Information about the Past, Present and Future Through*

Clairvoyance, by Sophia diGregorio.

To Divine the Outcome of an Event by
Means of a Pendulum

Divination by means of pendulum dowsing is one of the most practical and versatile ways of predicting the outcome of a future event. The application of the pendulum to gain information is a very simple one and you can devise all kinds of systems for determining answers based on the binary response of "Yes" or "No." Dowsing relies on the ability to read subtle energetic signals. You will be able to do this remarkably well with a little practice.

A pendulum is a small weight suspended from a string or chain. A ring on a string or a Luck Ball will suffice for your first efforts. But, if you become serious about pendulum dowsing, you should obtain a well balanced pendulum made from steel, carved gemstone or some other sturdy material.

If you have never used a pendulum before, the idea of dowsing may seem strange or impossible. But, it is a perfectly natural ability and one that many educated people take very seriously. In fact, the American Society of Dowsers (www.dowsers.org) is a nationwide organization that teaches people how to dowse with pendulums and other devices to obtain accurate information about the location of water, minerals and other resources. A similar organization, the British Society of Dowsers, exists in the U.K. (www.britishdowsers.org)

After you have selected a pendulum, perform a simple consecration ceremony. It is not necessary to do this to obtain good results with a pendulum, but you may find it helpful, especially if you are a first-time dowser.

Hold the pendulum in the palm of your left hand. With your right hand, make a few passes over the pendulum as if you are brushing it without actually touching it. As you do this, command any old energy to release and dissolve itself into the environment. You may, also, pass the pendulum through the purifying smoke of a White Sage bundle.

Then, hold the pendulum between both palms and say, 'I consecrate you to my service in the name of the Most High (or the God and Goddess) that you shall always give true answers to all my questions."

Now, you must program the pendulum. This is, also, a very simple procedure.

There are different ways to program a pendulum. You can hold it out in front of you and command it to show you the movements that mean "Yes" and "No" for you. Or, you can tell it which movement to make for these responses. For example, it is common to designate an up and down motion to mean "Yes" and a side to side motion to mean "No." Although, some people prefer to use circular motions where a clockwise motion means "Yes" and a counter-clockwise motion means "No."

Test your pendulum by asking it questions to which you already know the answer. For example, "Is my name John?" or "Is today Wednesday?"

After you have established the signals it will give you and tested them, use your pendulum to determine the winning numbers in the lottery. Choose a simple lottery game that asks for three to four numbers.

There are many different ways you can use the pendulum to determine the winning numbers for the next drawing.

One method is to create a chart or list of every possible winning number. Then, hold the pendulum over each number and ask if this is the winning number for that drawing on that date.

Sometimes people develop a bias for or against a particular number. If you feel this is occurring, try a method where the numbers are hidden from your physical sight. Write each possible winning number on a 1" x 1" square of colored or heavy paper. Place the pieces upside down and shuffle them. Then, use the same method with the pendulum, holding it over each square of paper and asking if this is the correct number for the upcoming drawing.

If you bet on the outcome of games or races, you may

use your pendulum in the same fashion to determine the winner. For example, hold it over the names or numbers of each entry in the race to determine which one will come in first place.

Formulate your question, then assume the mindset of a disinterested observer and allow the pendulum to give its answer. If you are having difficulty receiving accurate answers, consider how you worded your question. The pendulum is an extension of your subconscious mind, which takes your wording very literally. Therefore, word your questions precisely and unequivocally.

If you are still having difficulty, make sure you are sufficiently hydrated. If you are feeling tired or anxious, wait until you have rested and your mind is more serene and then try, again.

The future is not fixed, partly because other people are mentally and emotionally focused on their own desired outcomes of an event, which may influence the results. But, if you do an experiment involving guesses versus focused attempts to obtain information about the outcome of an event using a pendulum, you will likely find that the accuracy of pendulum results are far superior to mere guesses.

Beneficial Timing for Divination

You may find that you have better results with the pendulum at certain times. Psychic researchers have found that their experiments render more accurate results at a Local Sidereal Time of 13:30.

Local Sidereal Time (LST) is a method of calculating time that is used by astrologers to keep track of planetary movements. It is the time of Galactic Center Rising. It is, also, referred to as "Libra Time" because the constellation Libra is at 24 degrees and almost directly overhead.

This conclusion is documented by Dr. James P. Spottiswoode and Edwin C. May in, "Anomalous Cognition Effect Size: Dependence on Sidereal Time and Solar Wind Parameters," in *The Journal for Scientific*

Exploration. See this and other documentation at: http://www.jsasoc.com/library.html.

Determine your Local Sidereal Time by using a LST calculator or a sidereal clock. Free smart phone applications and software are now available online for this purpose. Also, calculate your Local Sidereal Time using your longitude at: http://tycho.usno.navy.mil/sidereal.html.

Spell to Influence the Outcome of an Event

To influence the outcome of an event, you must intensely focus your intention. If you have used divination to determine the outcome, you may use this spell to stabilize the future event or to influence it in some other way.

You will need the following:

White candle
8 small Quartz crystals
Piece of plain paper
Black or blue ink pen

On the paper, draw a circle 1 1/2 to 2" in diameter. Then, draw eight smaller circles in an arrangement around this circle, approximately 2 to 3" away from the one in the center. The arrangement of these circles should be like the points on a compass at north, south, east and west, with a circle in between each of these points at northeast, southeast, southwest and northwest.

Then, draw lines from each of these smaller circles to the larger one. So, the end result looks like a circle in the middle with eight, equidistant spokes around it, each terminating in a small circle. This does not have to be perfect, but the lines you draw between the larger circle and each of the smaller ones should be continuous and unbroken.

Place a representation of the thing you would like to influence in the center of the circle. This may be an entry ticket to a sweepstake, a ticket for a lottery drawing or a winning arrangement of poker cards. Alternatively, write the time and place of an event and the specific outcome you desire on a small piece of plain, white paper and place this in the center circle.

Place the candle on top of the item in the center circle. Place a small crystal in each of the eight smaller circles surrounding it.

Then, light the candle. Charge the crystals and impregnate this energy with your desired outcome. Allow the candle to burn down completely.

The ink lines act like an antenna along which the magnified energy from the crystals flows in toward the center of this design. This arrangement functions as a broadcast center for your intention.

This system works for other situations or even people you want to influence.

Prayer to the Apsarâs for Success in Gambling

The Apsarâs are a group of shape-shifting, female cloud spirits of India who rule over good fortune and gambling. They are very beautiful dancing spirits who are similar to the muses of ancient Greece. Before gambling, call upon these spirits to influence the outcome in your favor.

"The successful, victorious, skilfully gaming Apsarâ, that Apsarâ who makes the winnings in the game of dice, do I call hither. The skilfully gaming Apsarâ who sweeps and heaps up the stakes, that Apsarâ who takes the winnings in the game of dice, do I call hither. May she, who dances about with the dice, when she takes the stakes from the game of dice, when she desires to win for us, obtain the advantage by her magic! May she come to us full of abundance! Let them not win this wealth of ours! The Apsarâs who rejoice in dice, who carry grief and wrath that joyful and exulting Apsarâ, do I call hither."[15]

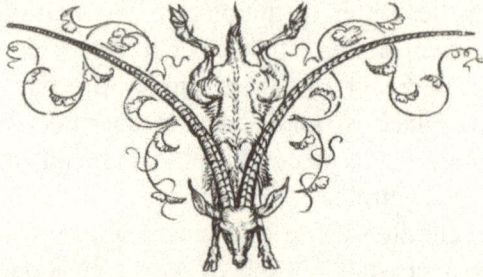

Hindu Prayer for Success at Dice Games

Indra is the supreme king of the Hindu devas who is a fiery god of war and thunder. Maghavan is one of his names and the Maruts are his servants. Call upon his power for success in dice games.

Before gambling, recite the following prayer from the *Hymns of the Atharva-Veda*:

"As the lightning at all times smites irresistibly the tree, thus would I today irresistibly beat the gamesters with my dice! Whether they be alert, or not alert, the fortune of these folks, unresisting, shall assemble from all sides, the gain within my hands! I invoke with reverence Agni, who has his own riches; here attached he shall heap up gain for us! I procure wealth for myself, as if with chariots that win the race. May I accomplish auspiciously the song of praise to the Maruts! May we by thy aid conquer the adversary; help us to obtain our share in every contest! Make for us, O Indra, a good and ample road; crush, O Maghavan, the lusty power of our enemies! I have conquered and cleaned thee out; I have also gained thy reserve. As the wolf plucks to pieces the sheep, thus do I pluck thy winnings. Even the strong hand the bold player conquers, as the skilled gambler heaps up his winnings at the proper time. Upon him that loves the game and does not spare his money, the game verily bestows the delights of wealth. Through the possession of cattle we all would suppress our wretched poverty, or with grain our hunger, O thou oft implored god! May we foremost among rulers, unharmed, gain wealth by our cunning devices! Gain is deposited in my right hand, victory in my left. Let me become a conqueror of cattle, horses, wealth, and gold! O dice, yield play, profitable as a cow that is rich in milk! Bind me to a streak of gain, as the bow is bound with the string!"[16]

12 SPELLS FOR WEALTH

Use these spells to achieve overflowing abundance, to acquire all of the material things you desire and to enjoy the fruits of your labor.

Hexagram Spell to Obtain Great Wealth

Use the life force generating power of the hexagram to obtain your desires. Within the hexagram can be found a representation of all the elements. It is a symbol of great power that will breathe life into your dreams of wealth.

You will need the following:

Piece of paper
White candle

Draw a hexagram on a white piece of paper. A hexagram is made by drawing a triangle the point up over the top of a triangle with its point down.

Take some time to think about all of the things you would like to buy without regard to cost. Maybe you would like a new house, car, jewelry or other luxuries. Let your imagination run wild.

Write all of your ideas in the center of the hexagram. Then choose the six most important ones and write one of them in each of the six small triangles that comprise your hexagram.

When you have finished this exercise, place the candle in its holder on top of the paper right in the middle of your hexagram. Light the candle and imagine your request going out to the universe. When the candle has burned down, bury the refuse and your request in your yard and forget about it.

King Midas Wealth Magnetization

According to the ancient Greek legend, King Midas loved gold so much that he made a prayer for more. His wish was granted and, thereafter, everything he touched turned to gold. The King Midas Touch Spell will not literally turn everything you touch to gold, but, it is intended to bring you good fortune in all of your financial affairs.

Perform this spell on a Sunday at sunrise during a waxing moon while facing eastward.

You will need the following:

Purification Bath (formula below)
King Midas Touch Oil (formula below)
Gold or yellow candle
Gold ring or pendant with a Sunstone setting or a Talisman of the Sun
Bowl of Sea Salt
Myrrh or Frankincense resin
Bowl of Water

Select a ring or pendant with a Sunstone setting, which will be consecrated and blessed in the following ceremony and worn as a talisman to bring you the golden touch of King Midas in all of your affairs.

Alternatively, there are numerous talismans of the sun to choose from such as the Seals of the Sun from the *Books of Moses* and the popular Pentacles of the Sun from *The Greater Key of Solomon*. They are commonly sold at online metaphysical stores. These talismans can, also, be fashioned with gold Precious Metal Clay. Gold is the color of the sun. It is the kingliest of the seven noble metals. Therefore, whatever you select should be made of gold or, at least, have a gold patina.

If you choose to make your own talisman, begin this operation at sunrise on Sunday. The following consecration ritual of the talisman should be conducted at this same planetary hour.

Before you begin the consecration ceremony, purify yourself with a bath.

Purification Bath

You will need the following:

1 gallon Water
1/2 cup of Rosemary
1/4 cup Bay Leaves
1/4 cup White Clover blossoms
1/4 cup Eucalyptus
2 to 3 cups of Sea Salt

Boil the above herbs in water to make a decoction. Allow the mixture to cool. Strain it. Then, add it along with the Sea Salt to a tub of water to make a purifying bath.

When you have finished bathing, return to your altar. Anoint the candle with King Midas Touch Oil, using a motion toward you.

King Midas Touch Oil

1 cup Sunflower oil
7 Basil leaves
2 T. Chamomile
2 T. Calendula
1 T. Myrrh
Gold ring or coin in the master bottle

Place the candle on the altar along with the talisman. Then, light the candle and stand in silence for a moment while visualizing a ball of white energy tinged with blue. Hold your hands a few inches apart with the palms facing inward. With your eyes closed, feel this ball energy between your palms. Move your palms toward each other, then apart as you form this ball of energy. When you can really feel it, place your hands over the talisman and push the ball of energy into it.

When this is done, pass it quickly near the flame of the fire and say, "I bless this talisman with the element of fire, in the name of the ancient and holy King of the Sun. So be it!"

Place the talisman before you, once again, and concentrate as before, with your eyes closed and the palms of your hands facing inward. Form a ball of swirling blue and green-tinged white light. When you can feel this energy very strongly between your palms, force it into the talisman.

When this is done, dip the talisman into the water and say, "I bless this talisman with the element of water, in the name of the ancient and holy King of the Sun. So be it!"

Again, place the talisman in front of you and focus as before. This time, between your palms see a ball of pure white light, which represents the balancing force of air. When you can feel this energy very strongly, force it into the talisman.

When this is done, pass the talisman through the smoke of Myrrh resin and say, "I bless this talisman with the element of air, in the name of the ancient and holy King of the Sun. So be it!"

Place the talisman in front of you, again. And hold your palms apart from each other in the same manner as before. This time, visualize a ball of dense, heavy energy of a yellow or brownish color that becomes denser and heavier in between your palms as you work with it. When you feel it very strongly and it is well formed, force this energy into the talisman.

When this is done, sprinkle the talisman with Salt and say, "I bless this talisman with the element of earth, in the name of the ancient and holy King of the Sun. So be it!"

When you have finished this entire procedure, anoint the talisman with King Midas Touch Oil and say:

"I bless and consecrate this talisman in the name of the most ancient and holy King of the Sun, that it shall be endowed with the power to bestow wealth upon me, so that every road I walk on is paved with bricks of gold and all I touch prospers and flourishes. So mote it be!"

Wear this talisman so that it is in contact with your skin.

Nine Wealthy Desires Knot Spell

Use this spell to manifest your desires for wealth.

You will need the following:

White string or cord (18" to 2' long)
9 white candles
Needle or thorn with which to make an inscription
Wishing Oil (formula below)
9 index cards
Piece of paper
Shoe box

Consider your life as you would like it to be without worrying about how you will achieve your goals. Right now, just think about your dreams for your ideal life.

Remember that wealth is about more than just making money. So, your future desires should include more than just this medium, but all the ways in which you plan to enjoy your life. This may include career, family and other goals, of which money is only a part.

After you have brainstormed on the piece of paper, divide the wishes up nine ways so that related ideas are divided into nine separate categories. Write each of these ideas on a separate index card.

Arrange your candles in their holders on the altar in three rows of three candles each. Place one of the index cards under each one. One by one, pick up each candle and inscribe one or two words into the side of it that comprise the basic idea of the desire written on its corresponding card. Do this for each one in succession.

Anoint each candle with Wishing Oil using a motion toward you as you do so, as if you are pulling these desires toward you.

Wishing Oil

1 cup Sunflower oil
3 T. Ginseng
3 Hazel nuts
3 T. Job's Tears
3 Peach pits
3 T. dried Periwinkle
9 Pomegranate seeds
3 T. Sage dried and powdered
Oil of 1 Vitamin E capsule as a preservative

Once this is done, light the first candle and read the wish written on the card associated with it. Then, tie a knot in the string and anoint it with a drop of Wishing Oil. Perform the same procedure with each candle in succession.

Allow the candles to burn down completely. Then, gather the cards, roll them up into a scroll and fasten it with the knotted string.

Place the scroll and the refuse from the candles into a

cardboard box and put it somewhere in your house, for example the attic or the basement, where you won't find it or think about it, again, for a long time.

Ritual Bath to Attract Luxuries

Use this bath spell to attract a luxurious lifestyle.

You will need the following:

4 purple, yellow or white votive candles
Wealthy Way Wash and Bath
1/4 cup White Vinegar
2 cups Sea Salt or Epsom Salts
Clean, white cleaning cloth

Make a gallon of strong tea using the Wealthy Way formula. Pour two cups of this potion into a plastic or metal container and add 1/4 cup of White Vinegar to it. Then, using a white cloth, clean every washable surface in your bathroom.

Light each of the candles and set them at the four corners of your bath tub. Draw yourself a bath and add the remainder of the potion and the Salt. As you bathe, envision the specific luxuries you want to attract into your life.

When you are finished with your bath, step out of the tub and dry off. Say, "I am now a new person. I live a life of luxury and all of the things I desire come to me easily and naturally."

Spell to Draw a Sugar Daddy or Sugar Mama

On a Sunday during a full moon, perform this spell to attract a wealthy benefactor.

You will need the following:

White candle
Needle or thorn with which to make an inscription
Sugar Daddy or Sugar Mama Oil (formula below)
Copal resin
Thyme, dried
Piece of paper
Red mojo bag
Fire safe container

Inscribe your name on the side of the candle. Then, anoint it with Sugar Daddy or Sugar Mama Oil using a motion toward you.

Sugar Daddy or Sugar Mama Oil

1 cup Almond oil
1 T. Coltsfoot
1 T. Cloves
2 T. Orris root
1 T. Poppy seeds
2 T. Snake Root
2 T. Violet

A few drops of this oil may, also, be worn and used in a meditative baths to help draw the situation you desire.

On a clean piece of white paper, write a message to your Sugar Daddy or Sugar Mama, as if you were writing a personal letter. Search your heart. Tell him or her that you are ready for them to come into your life. Describe what you would like from this relationship and what you plan to offer in return.

Fold the paper toward you once. Turn it 90 degrees and

fold it toward you, again.

Burn equal parts of Copal and Thyme as an incense and pass the paper through the smoke while reciting the following incantation:

"Goddess of Good Fortune, smile upon me and unite me with a generous friend, so that we may be a blessing to each other."

Do this three times while focusing all your energy on drawing this situation to you.

Place one tablespoon each of Copal and Thyme into a mojo bag along with the note. Keep it with you for nine consecutive days.

On the ninth day, again, burn the herbs in the bag as incense. Pass the paper through the smoke and recite the above incantation three times. Afterward, burn the note in a fire safe container to release your request into the cosmos.

Spell to Attract a Wealthy Husband or Wife

To attract a wealthy husband or wife, begin this spell on a Sunday during a waxing moon.

You will need the following:

White Bride and Groom figure candle
Wealthy Wife or Wealthy Husband Oil (formula below)
Piece of paper
Bag or small box

If you cannot obtain a Bride and Groom figure candle, substitute two white human figure candles or two plain white candles.

Do some soul searching about what your ideal mate would be like and what each of you would bring to a romantic partnership.

Then, on a clean piece of paper list each of the qualities you desire. To the bottom of the page, add the words, "Bring my beloved wife (or husband) to me."

Anoint the edges of this paper with a few drops of Wealthy Wife or Wealthy Husband Oil.

Wealthy Wife or Wealthy Husband Oil
Use this oil to attract a wealthy spouse

1 cup Almond oil
1 T. Basil
1 T. Camellia
1 T. Dittany of Crete
1 T. Elder bark
1 T. Violet
Lodestone
Orris root (optional)
High John the Conqueror root (optional)

Women may add Orris root to the mixture, which is, also, used to inspire generosity in others. Men may add High John the Conqueror root. The most important ingredients in this formula are Elder bark and Violet.

If you are using a Bride and Groom candle, carve out a space in the bottom. Place the paper inside the space and place the candle in its holder. If you are using another type of candle, fold your paper toward you once or twice and place it beneath the candle holder.

Light the candle and sit quietly meditating on your wish for this relationship. Concentrate on the flame of the candle and see it sending the message you wrote on the paper out into the universe. Allow the candle to burn out.

Alternatively, let it burn for a little while before snuffing it out over the course of nine consecutive nights.

When the candle is completely burned out. Place the refuse from this spell into a bag or box and bury it in your yard or hide it where it won't be found or thought of again for a very long time.

Wealthy Friends Attraction Spell

There is a lot of truth in the saying, "It's not what you know, but who you know that matters." It is, also, true that people tend to be a lot like their friends. Chances are if your friends are wealthy and successful, you will be, too. This spell to attract wealthy friends is intended to help you soar among the eagles. It is best performed on a Sunday at sunrise during a waxing moon.

You will need the following:

Golden Eagle statue or image
Hair or bodily fluid
2' long white ribbon
2' long golden ribbon
2' long purple ribbon
White candle
Gold candle
Purple candle
Needle or thorn with which to make an inscription
Drawing Oil
Adhesive tape
2 Lodestones
Gold magnetic sand
A red mojo bag

Inscribe your name and the three words, "Fides, Sancus, Fama," which are the names of three ancient gods and goddesses of trust, loyalty and fame, onto each candle. Anoint each one with Drawing Oil in a motion toward you while imaging the gift of wealthy friendships coming to you.

Arrange your altar with the eagle and three candles. Place the golden candle in front of the eagle, the white one to his left and the purple one to his right.

On the white ribbon, write, "Fides." On the golden one, write, "Sancus." On the purple one, write, "Fama." Then, make a knot in the end, binding these three strands together. If your hair is long enough, incorporate a few strands into this knot. Otherwise, add your saliva or a drop of your blood. As you knot this end, meditate on your desire for wealthy, influential friends who will help you achieve your dreams.

Fasten the ribbon to the image of the eagle or on the altar near its feet with the piece of adhesive tape.

Braid each strand repeating the following incantation with each motion of over or under: "I draw and bind under me the powers of Fides, Sancus and Fama."

When you reach the end of the braid, tie a final knot in all three strands.

Then, light each candle in succession, repeating the following prayer, each time:

"Brother Eagle, King of the Sky, who communes with the gods, hear me and answer my prayer. Bless me with your spirit that I may have your protection and know your powers for myself. Give me a clear vision for the future and help me to move upward, soaring ever higher, into the society of the wealthy, powerful and successful, that I may partake of these fruits. Thank you, Brother Eagle. Amen."

Allow these candles to burn down while you consider the powers of the eagle. He is the king of birds, a spirit of the sun and a representation of the crowning glory of success. Fierce in battle, the eagle protects from evil and he has a clear vision for the future.

Meditate on your desires. Allow your imagination to run wild. Do not try to work out how you will find the friends you desire, only focus on drawing them to you.

When the candles have burned down, take the ribbon and

place it in a mojo bag. Anoint two small Lodestones with Drawing Oil and add them to the bag. Feed them with a pinch of gold magnetic sand. Carry this with you at all times to attract the powerful, influential friends you desire.

Yellow Buddha for Wealth

The yellow aspect of Buddha is called "Dzambhala." He is the Buddha of wealth.

Inside your home, place four yellow Buddha statues facing inward at each of the four cardinal directions to draw wealth.

Chant the following mantra 108 times:

"Aum Dzambhala Djardin Djaya Soha."

The following is an English approximation of the sounds:

"Aum Zahm-bah-lah Jar-din Dah-yah Swah-ha."

13 CALLING UPON SPIRITS, SAINTS, GODS AND GODDESSES

Calling upon spirits is another way to empower your spells and achieve your goals, whether it is to make money, obtain good fortune, build wealth or succeed at gambling. Establishing a relationship with a powerful spirit is one of the most effective means of gaining control of your destiny. It doesn't matter which spirit you call upon as long as you choose one you feel comfortable with who possesses abilities compatible with your goals.

Angelic Help

Angels are spirits that existed in primordial times, which have never lived as human beings. Although many Westerners may associate them with Christianity, they are known throughout the world, from the most ancient documents and civilizations, as the earliest of existing beings. When they are considered broadly, they include nature spirits, creative spirits from primeval existence and beings of both the light and the darkness. There are numerous types of angels and systems of classifying them.

According to ancient lore, the names of the angels are other "names of god," each endowed with special powers.

Angels are co-creators with a non-anthropomorphic creative force. When they appear to the clairvoyant, they take on a discernible human-like shape. Like fallen angels, they can alter their appearance at will. They are similar to the light-radiating devas or nature spirits of the Hindus who are spiritual messengers and assistants to mankind.

Among the most powerful of angels are the archangels.

The Archangel Michael is a warrior and fierce protector, usually depicted wearing red and blue, a shield in one hand and a sword in the other as he slays a demon or dragon beneath his feet. His day of the week is Sunday and his Feast Day is September 29th. He is a powerful fixture in Mexican witchcraft and is employed by healers and exorcists for protection from all evil. Michael destroys adversarial forces and keeps those who call upon him safe from harm. He will protect your home and business and keep you safe during travel. Pray to Michael as follows:

"O Powerful and Glorious Archangel Michael, guard my home and place of business and protect me from all harm as I journey by land, sea and air."

The Archangel Gabriel helps you to keep a positive attitude during difficult times and to obtain the things you need. His day of the week is Monday and his Feast Day is March 24th. Pray to Gabriel as follows:

"O Archangel Gabriel, please, grant me your comfort and consolation at this time of difficulty and obtain for me all of the things that I need."

The Archangel Raphael helps you to keep food on the table. His day of the week is Tuesday and his feast Day is October 24th. If you are impoverished and worry about not being able to feed yourself or your family, call upon him for help. Pray to Raphael as follows:

"O Glorious Archangel Raphael, great prince of the heavenly court, you are known for your wisdom and grace.

Be a guide to me and my family and protect us from poverty and hunger. Let there always be nourishing food on our table."

The Archangel Uriel is the angel of justice and healing. Resolve problems with co-workers or relationships that are interfering with your ability to earn a living by contacting him for help. His day of the week is Wednesday and his Feast Day is July 28th. Pray to Uriel as follows:

"O Archangel Uriel, shine your light on my life and guide me to find solutions to the difficulties I face. Use your power to bring harmony to my life and remove all sources of conflict."

The Archangel Barakiel is the angel of good fortune who will help you, even in the most difficult situations. He is a prince of the spiritual realm called the Second Heaven and his day of the week is Saturday. His name means "Lightning of God" or "God's Blessing." He is, also, called Barbiel, Barbuel and Baruel. His sign is Pisces and he rules over the month of February.

Call upon Barakiel to bring you inspiration, creativity and the power of discernment. Also, call upon him when you are gambling and really want to win. Pray to Barakiel as follows:

"O Prince Barakiel, Angel of Good Fortune, assist me by swiftly bringing inspiration, good luck and abundance into my life."

The Archangel Zadkiel is an angel of freedom and benevolence. Invoke his assistance to find creative solutions to your business and financial problems. He is associated with the color violet and the planet Jupiter. Pray to Zadkiel as follows:

"O Archangel Zadkiel, I call upon your power to destroy all strife and to promote peace and harmony. Inspire me with creativity and illuminate the darkness with your holy spirit that I may find solutions to all of my problems."

When an angel's Feast Day is unknown, it may be celebrated on September 29th, which is the day of all angels. Ask for help aloud or silently, addressing the angel by name. A well-developed clairvoyant may be able to see an angel in its astral form.

There are many other ways to contact powerful angels. A method for summoning a particular class of angels based on timing is given in the *Ars Almadel*, which is the 4th Book of the *Lesser Key of Solomon*. An Almadel is a talisman made of white wax. The angels are called by using three grains of Mastic tree resin on a piece of charcoal as incense. The invocation of the angels is done at sunrise on Sunday.

The *Ars Almadel* specifies that the talisman, four candles and the support for the talisman in the form of an altar, which is a base or "foot," should be made of the same pure, white wax. Certain angels can only be made to manifest at certain times of the year depending on their rank or "altitude."

A specific prayer is given to call and communicate with the angels when they manifest, however, you may use a similar prayer in your mental communications with them:

"O thou mighty and blessed Angel N., I, the servant of the same thy God, do entreat and humbly beseech thee to come and show unto me all things that I shall desire of thee, subject to the power of thine office and the good Pleasure of the Lord our God. By the three names of the true God, ADONAI, HELOMI, PINE, and by the name ANA BONA, I beseech and constrain thee forthwith to appear visibly in thy proper shape, speaking in my ears audibly, that I may have thy blessed, angelical and glorious assistance, familiar friendship, constant society, communication and instruction, now and at all times, herein and in all truths which the Almighty God, King of Kings, Giver of all good gifts, shall be graciously pleased to bestow on me. Therefore, O thou blessed Angel N., be friendly unto me, do for me as God hath empowered thee, whereunto I now adjure thee to appear it; power and presence, that I may sing with His Holy Angels O MAPPA LAMAN, HALLELUJAH. AMEN."

Angels pre-date the major world religions of Christianity, Islam and Judaism. Members of oldest known, continuously existing religion on earth, that of the Yazidis of Iraq, revere a benevolent creator angel similar to Lucifer. Furthermore, according to legend, King Solomon obtained his knowledge, power and great wealth through his communication with angels, including the fallen ones and their offspring.

Demonic Help

Demons are the offspring of fallen angels who are likewise servants to mankind, although some of them are reluctant and must be persuaded. Some of these entities who are commonly referred to as demons are, in fact, the fallen angels, themselves. Once they are summoned and some rapport is established they can be induced to help you by giving you ideas or information about obtaining money and wealth and to serve you in other ways according to their individual nature.

Numerous Goetic demons have the power to locate treasure for the conjurer, to give counsel or to tell the location of lost or stolen items, among other services. The following are names of helpful spirits from the *Ars Goetia of The Lesser Key of Solomon*: Seere, Valac, Cimeies, Gremory, Amy or Avnas, Purson, Barbatos, Astarot, and Foras.[17]

A Classical Conjuring Circle and Triangle

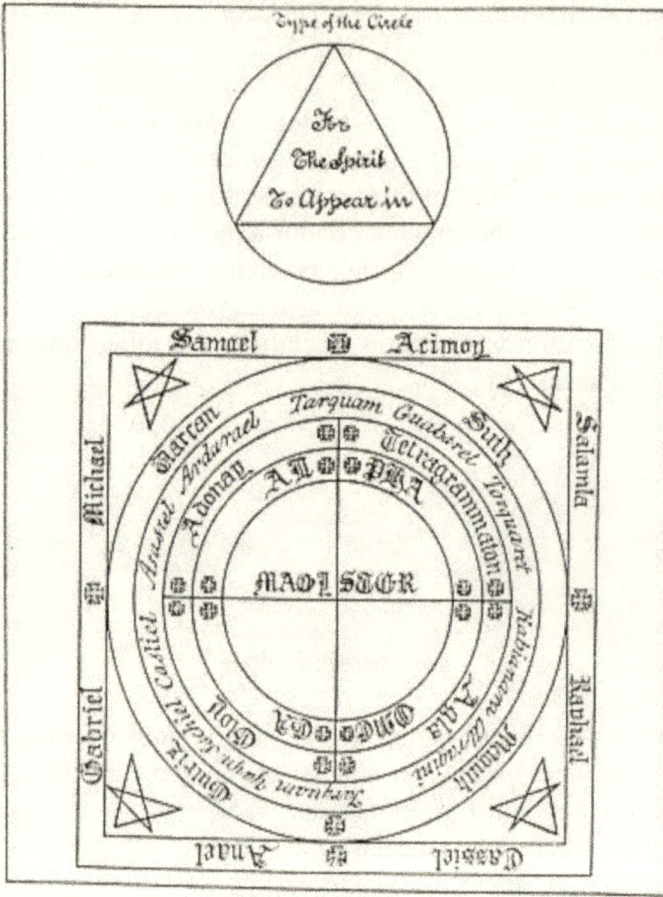

Some of these beings, for example Seere, are of a good nature, but others can be unpleasant and difficult to control once they are summoned. Therefore, the conjurer casts a circle from which to safely and effectively converse with the demon. Likewise, the demon is contained in its own circle or triangle wherein he can be tamed and instructed. Both the circle and the triangle should be constructed with the idea in mind that they exist both physically and in an infinite number of spiritual realms.

As discussed in the chapter on clearing space, there is no

particular procedure for constructing the circle and a simple one will suffice as long as you understand that you stand inside it as a master of the infinite. If you are familiar with it, as many people are, then even a Wiccan-style circle will serve you, although Wiccans typically do not acknowledge the existence of dark entities and do not work with them. You should have a circle, regardless, and from it you must see yourself as god operating from within it. It can be as simple as a circle drawn on the floor or marked out with tape.

Each of the aforementioned beings has its own sigil, which can be found in the *Lesser Key of Solomon*. The sigil acts as a kind of antenna for the spirit and carries its individual harmonic signature. It is placed inside the magical triangle. Talismans may be constructed of paper and ink, however, you can now easily construct metal talismans of silver, gold and bronze using Precious Metal Clay, which is available at hobby shops or online.

Inside the triangle, you may, also, place an offering to the spirit in the form of Devil's Pod or Bat Nut (Trapa Bicornus), which are seed pods used as offerings to dark spirits.

Alternatively, make an offering of incense to the spirits using 2 parts Cinnamon and 2 parts Calamus root combined with 1 part Myrrh and 1 part Cassia. This incensed is based on Abramelin Oil, which is used to provide an environment conducive to spirit manifestation.

Below are the first, second and third conjurations of the spirit and the license to depart. If you have highly developed visualization skills, this conjuration can, also, be performed mentally.

The Rite of Conjuration from the Lemegeton

On any day except "the second, fourth, sixth, ninth, tenth, twelfth or fourteenth" day of a new moon, perform the following ritual according to the *Lesser Key of Solomon*. A large amount of concentrated life force energy is required to supply sufficient energy for the demon to manifest more physically. For this reason, two or three people often perform these rites together. Sometimes conjurers place a bowl of water or something reflective into the triangle to assist the demon with manifestation.

The capitalized words in the conjuration are important names of power or names of "god," which are especially important to the operation. It is not necessary for you to believe in these gods, as such. They may or may not be representations of anthropomorphic beings, but their names contain power, which is why they should be sung and not just abruptly spoken.

When you see "N.," insert the name of the demon you wish to conjure. When you pronounce the words, do so carefully, syllable by syllable and draw the sounds out similar to the manner of a Catholic Priest reciting prayers at a mass.

The First Conjuration

"I invoke and conjure thee, O Spirit N., and, fortified with the power of the Supreme Majesty, I strongly command thee by BARALAMENSIS, BALDACHIENSIS, PAUMACHIE, APOLORESEDES and the most potent princes GENIO, LIACHIDE, Ministers of the Tartarean Seat, chief princes of the seat of APOLOGIA in the ninth region; I exorcise and command thee, O Spirit N., by Him Who spoke and it was done, by the Most Holy and glorious Names ADONAI, EL, ELOHIM, ELOHE, ZEBAOTH, ELION, ESCHERCE, JAH, TETRAGRAMMATON, SADAI: do thou forthwith appear and show thyself unto me, here before this circle, in a fair and human shape, without any deformity or horror; do thou come forthwith, from whatever part of the world, and make rational answers to my questions; come presently, come visibly, come affably, manifest that which I desire, being conjured by the Name of the Eternal, Living and True God, HELIOREM; I conjure thee also by the particular and true Name of thy God to whom thou owest thine obedience; by the name of the King who rules over thee, do thou come without tarrying; come, fulfill my desires; persist unto the end, according, to my intentions."

"I conjure thee by Him to Whom all creatures are obedient, by this ineffable Name, TETRAGRAMMATON JEHOVAH, by which the elements are overthrown, the air is shaken, the sea turns back, the fire is generated, the earth moves and all the hosts of things celestial, of things terrestrial, of things infernal, do tremble and are confounded together; speak unto me visibly and affably in a clear, intelligible voice, free from ambiguity. Come therefore in the name ADONAI ZEBAOTH; come, why dost thou tarry? ADONAI SADAY, King of kings, commands thee."

A conjuration of this kind requires patience and persistence to produce results. Repeat the previous two paragraphs several times and if this fails, go on to the next part, as follows:

Second Conjuration

The name "AGLA" is pronounced like "Ah-Gah-Lah."

"I invoke, conjure and command thee, O Spirit N., to appear and show thyself visibly before this circle, in fair and comely shape, without deformity or guile, by the Name of ON; by the Name Y and V, which Adam heard and spake; by the Name of JOTH, which Jacob learned from the Angel on the night of his wresting and was delivered from the hands of his brother Esau; by the Name of God AGLA, which Lot heard and was saved with his family; by the Name ANEHEXETON, which Aaron spake and was made wise; by the Name SCHEMES AMATHIA, which Joshua invoked and the Sun stayed upon his course; by the Name EMMANUEL, which the three children, Shadrach, Meshach and Abednego, chanted in the midst of the fiery furnace, and they were delivered; by the Name ALPHA and OMEGA, which Daniel uttered, and destroyed Bel and the Dragon; by the Name ZEBAOTH, which Moses named, and all the rivers and waters in the land of Egypt brought forth frogs, which ascended into the houses of the Egyptians, destroying all things; by the Name ESCERCHIE ARISTON, which also Moses named, and the rivers and waters in the land of Egypt were turned into blood; by the Name ELION, on which Moses called, and there fell a great hail, such as never was seen since the creation of the world; by the Name ADONAI, which Moses named, and there came up locusts over all the land of Egypt and devoured what the hail had left; by the Name HAGIOS, by the Seal of ADONAI, by those others, which are JETROS, ATHENOROS, PARACLETUS; by the three Holy and Secret Names, AGLA, ON, TETRAGRAM-MATON; by the dreadful Day of Judgment; by the changing Sea of Glass which is before the face of the Divine Majesty, mighty and powerful; by the four beasts before the Throne, having eyes before and behind; by the fire which is about the Throne, by the Holy Angels of Heaven, by the Highly Wisdom of God; by the Seat of BASDATHEA, by this Name PRIMEMATUM, which Moses named, and the earth opened and swallowed Corah, Dathan and Abiram; do thou make faithful answers unto all my demands, and perform all my desires, so far as thine office shall permit. Come therefore peaceably and affably; come visibly and without delay; manifest that which I desire; speak with a clear and intelligible voice, that I may understand thee."

If you still fail to achieve results after the Second Conjuration, move on to the Third Conjuration, as follows:

Third Conjuration

"I conjure thee, O spirit N., by all the most glorious and efficacious Names of the Great and Incomparable Lord the God of Hosts, come quickly and without delay, front whatsoever part of the world thou art in; make rational answers to my demands; come visibly, speak affably, speak intelligibly to my understanding. I conjure and constrain thee, O Spirit N., by all the aforesaid Names, as also by those seven other Names wherewith Solomon bound thee and thy fellows in the brazen vessels to wit, ADONAI, PRERAI, TETRAGRAMMATON, ANEXHEXETON, INESSENSATOAL, PATHUMATON and ITEMON; do thou manifest before this circle, fulfill my will in all things that may seem good to me. Be disobedient, refuse to come, and by the power of the Supreme Being, the everlasting Lord, that God Who created thee and me, the whole world, with all contained therein, in the space of six days; by EYE, by SARAY, by the virtue of the Name PRIMEMATUM, which commands the whole host of Heaven; be disobedient, and behold I will curse and deceive thee of thine office, thy joy and thy place; I will bind thee in the depths of the bottomless pit, there to remain until the Day of the Last judgment. I will chain thee in the Lake of Eternal Fire, in the Lake of Fire and Brimstone, unless thou come quickly, appearing before this circle, to do my will Come, therefore, in the Holy Names ADONAI, ZEBAOTH, AMIORAM; come, ADONAI commands thee."

According to the *Lesser Key of Solomon*, "Should he still fail to appear, you may be sure that he has been sent by his King to some other place. Invoke, therefore, the King to dispatch his servant."

In this case, invoke the king, as follows:

Invocation of the King

"O THOU great, powerful, and mighty KING AMAIMON, who bearest rule by the power of the SUPREME GOD EL over all spirits both superior and inferior of the Infernal Orders in the Dominion of the East; I do invoke and command thee by the especial and true name Of GOD; and by that God that Thou Worshippest; and by the Seal of thy creation; and by the most mighty and powerful name Of GOD, IEHOVAH TETRAGRAM-MATON who cast thee out of heaven with all other infernal spirits; and by all the most powerful and great names of GOD who created Heaven, and Earth, and Hell, and all things in them contained; and by their power and virtue; and by the name PRIMEUMATON who commandeth the whole host of Heaven; that thou mayest cause, enforce, and compel the Spirit N. to come unto me here before this Circle in a fair and comely shape, without harm unto me or unto any other creature, to answer truly and faithfully unto all my requests; so that I may accomplish my will and desire in knowing or obtaining any matter or thing which by office thou knowest is proper for him to perform or accomplish, through the power of GOD, EL, Who created and doth dispose of all things both celestial, aërial, terrestrial, and infernal."

Repeat the Invocation of the King two or three times. Afterward, conjure the spirit, again, beginning with the recitation of the First Conjuration, repeating each conjuration in succession two or three times. If this fails, the *Key of Solomon* provides methods of coercing and threatening a disobedient spirit to do your will, however, whenever you have more than one option, you should try to choose the most cooperative spirit for your purpose.

The manner in which you address the spirits should be commanding and in no way humble. As you recite your incantations, remember that you are the master and they are your servants.

Successful conjuration often requires patience and tenacity. It is, also, important to consider the matter of timing and to repeat the conjurations often and at varying times. Make notes of the success or failure of your experiments with regard to technique and timing.

If all attempts at spirit manifestation fail, try adding several drops of Simple Fluid Condenser to the bowl of water inside the triangle. A fluid condenser is a simple formula that helps the spirit form an etheric and more densely physical body.

Simple Fluid Condenser

This is a simple version of a fluid condenser adapted from the one given in the brilliant Czech occultist Franz Bardon's book, *Initiation into Hermetics*.[18] A similar formula is mentioned by Sybil Leek in her book, *Cast Your Own Spell*. It is used to condense the etheric field for manifestation in operations involving summoning. It, also, sustains the vibrational imprint placed upon it by the sorcerer.

Ingredients:

1/4 cup Chamomile (substitute Arnica, Life Everlasting or Lily blossoms)
1 to 2 quarts of Distilled Water
Several drops of blood or sperm
Vodka, Everclear or other grain alcohol

Begin by boiling the herb in approximately one quart of water. Lower the heat to a high simmer for 20 minutes, watching very carefully to make sure that the liquid doesn't evaporate and scorch the pot. Add more water as necessary. Reduce the liquid to approximately 1/4 cup or 50 ml.

Allow it to cool. Then, strain it and place it in a glass bottle. Add about a tablespoon of Everclear grain alcohol or Vodka as a preservative. Then, add 10 drops blood or sperm.

Place the lid on tightly and always shake the bottle before using it. When it is stored in a dark, cool place, it does not lose its strength for a few years.

Fluid condensers for various purposes along with instruction in evocation is given by Franz Bardon in *Initiation Into Hermetics: A Course of Instruction of Magic Theory & Practice* and *The Practice of Magical Evocation.*

Charge this condenser, just as you would charge any other object. Then, add several drops to the water in the triangle and begin the conjuration, again.

License to Depart

Whether you believe your conjuration was successful or not, it is wise to command the spirit to leave at the end of the session. Because of the possibility of beings lingering after such an operation as this, some magicians opt to perform the conjuration at a distance from their homes and beyond, at least, one crossroad or flowing water.

The License to Depart is as follows:

"O Spirit N., because thou hast diligently answered my demands, I do hereby license thee to depart, without injury to man or beast. Depart, I say, and be thou willing and ready to come, whensoever duly exorcised and conjured by the Sacred Rites of Magic. I conjure thee to withdraw peaceably and quietly, and may the peace of God continue for ever between me and thee. Amen."

After the License to Depart has been made, remain in the circle for a few minutes, while continuing to make prayers, to give the spirit time to leave. Afterward, if the circle has been drawn outside, it should be destroyed. If it has been drawn inside the house, then it may remain, although it should be done in a special room to which the door can be closed and people should not permitted to walk through it.

Furthermore, with regard to pacts, some entities may try to persuade you to make some kind of bilateral agreement with them, but this is not necessary. It is the duty of the spirits to serve mankind. You may make a gift to persuade the spirit to appear, but you must always remember that your position in relation to the spirit is a superior one.

The Faustian Spirit Aciel

Another interesting servant of mankind who is of interest to anyone seeking riches is named in Manly P. Hall's book, *The Secret Teachings of All Ages*, in a reference to the original source of the legend of Faust. The fallen angel

Aciel or Aziel is "the mightiest among those who serve men. He manifests in pleasing human form about three feet high. He must be invoked three times before he will come forth into the circle prepared for him. He will furnish riches and will instantly fetch things from a great distance, according to the will of the magician. He is as swift as human thought."[19]

This Faustian excerpt mentions the importance of timing, although it isn't specific about the day of the week upon which Aciel should be invoked. Three concentric circles with a cross in the center are drawn with a sword, which has caused no harm to anyone, just before sunrise. It gives a conjuration procedure similar to the one previously described.

Learn more about the invocation of Aciel from the book, *The Black Raven: Doctor Johannes Faust's Miracle and Magic Book*, attributed to Faust and translated into English by Karl Hans Welz (magitech.com/faust/introfst.html).

Help from the Saints

Various saints, some sanctioned by the Catholic Church and some not, may be called upon to help fulfill specific needs. Most saints are the spirits of spiritually advanced dead people, however, some the most powerful among them are folk saints who may or may not be spirits of the dead.

The basic procedure for calling upon any of the saints involves using images, candles, prayers, petitions, incense and oils. Place the image of a saint on your altar, anoint a candle with oil, light it and begin your prayer and make your petition. The burning of candles and incense are a form of offering to a saint. You may, also, make a small offering in the form of food, beverages or other items associated with the particular saint.

Most saints have their own corresponding prayers that incorporate information about their sainthood, however, you may pray to and petition them any way you like. For example, you may say something as simple as the following:

"Holy Saint N., I implore you to obtain for me [state your petition]. Please, grant my request."

Make a petition to a saint by writing your request on a little piece of paper, which you may place beneath the candle as it burns or beneath the image of the saint.

Make your prayers and petitions any day of the week or year, but note that certain days are favored by certain saints. These are the most propitious times to make your requests.

Very powerful prayers to the saints are conducted in the form of novenas. This is a series of prayers recited over a period of nine days.

Dress your altar and use colors corresponding with the particular saint or the type of request you are making. The following oil may be used with any of the saints:

All Saints Oil

2 cups Almond oil
7 drops White Peony
3 drops Cinnamon
3 drops Patchouli
3 drops Vanilla
7 drops Lavender
3 drops Gardenia
3 drops Vetivert

This oil is designed to enhance your psychic abilities and help you connect with the spirit realm. Apply it as a dressing to candles.

St. Anthony of Padua

St. Anthony of Padua helps you to overcome economic difficulties, to make the right financial decisions, find employment, improve your luck and restore lost money, wealth and opportunities. His day is June 13th, his day of the week is Tuesday and his color is brown or green. His symbol is the lily and bread is traditionally offered to him upon the altar.

Obtain a St. Anthony of Padua 7-day candle or an image of him along with a brown or green candle. Anoint the candle with Rue oil or Money Drawing Oil. Light it and say the Unfailing Prayer to St. Anthony, inserting your request, as follows:

"Blessed be God in His Angels and in His Saints. O Holy St. Anthony, gentlest of Saints, your love for God and Charity for His creatures made you worthy, when on earth, to possess miraculous powers. Encouraged by this thought, I implore you to obtain for me [state your petition]. O gentle and loving St. Anthony, whose heart was ever full of human sympathy, whisper my petition into the ears of the sweet Infant Jesus, who loved to be folded in your arms; and the gratitude of my heart will ever be yours. Amen."

Afterward, recite each of the following prayers thirteen times in succession: Our Father, Hail Mary, and Glory Be.

If you are seeking employment or trying to land a contract, appeal to St. Anthony's powers by way of a magical talisman consecrated to him.

You will need the following:

Image of St. Anthony
Green or brown candle
Two-dollar bill or other paper money
Rue oil
Cactus oil
Cinnamon oil
Red mojo bag

Light a candle to St. Anthony, then anoint the bill with equal parts of Rue oil, Cactus oil (Nopal Cactus or other) and Cinnamon oil. Hold the bill long ways and fold it toward you nine times. The first three times, the bill is facing you and you fold it down longways. Turn the bill 90 degrees and fold it three more times. Repeat for the last three. Always fold it in a motion toward yourself. As you do this recite the Unfailing Prayer to St. Anthony, promising him that you will give to the poor, if he helps you.

Place this bill in a little red mojo bag or wrap it in red flannel and carry it with you as you search for work.

St. Expedite

St. Expedite, also known as St. Expeditus, is an unofficial Catholic saint. The date of his birth is unknown, but it is believed he was martyred on April 19th in the year 303 A.D. in Melitene, Turkey. Little is known about the man behind the legend of St. Expedite, but he is supposed to have been a Roman Centurion who was killed by decapitation.

The term "expiditus" refers to a type of Roman soldier who traveled lightly and moved swiftly. He is generally portrayed with a palm leaf to denote that he is a martyr. He holds a cross in one hand with the word "Hodie," which is Latin for "today," written upon it. His foot crushes a crow who speaks the word "Cras," which is Latin for "tomorrow."

St. Expedite is often employed to speed the action of any working and to obtain whatever you need very quickly. He is the patron saint of shopkeepers who, also, presides over business transactions and legal matters. He helps his petitioners find quick solutions to problems of any kind.

Because he lost his head, he is something of a dullard who can easily become confused. Therefore, he must be petitioned very specifically, otherwise, he may misunderstand your request. Promises made to him must be swiftly kept as soon as he has performed his assigned task. If, promises to him are not kept quickly enough, he will withdraw the favor, sometimes with very unpleasant consequences to the spell caster. According to some, if you do not keep your end of the bargain, he will take the life of one of your family members as payment.

St. Expedite does not care about the nature of a request, he will carry it out according to the instructions he is given. He can be employed for any purpose, whatsoever, without regard to the nature of the task. Ask him to help you with a debt, a legal problem, a business negotiation or for gambling success.

His favorite color is red, but yellow and white are, also, used on his altar. His preferred day is Thursday, but you may work with him successfully on Tuesday and Wednesday, too. Make offerings to him in numbers of three. To work with St. Expedite, dress your altar in these colors and choose one of these days to begin your work.

You will need the following:

Red, white or yellow altar cloth
Image of St. Expedite
Red, white or yellow candle
Piece of paper
St. Expedite Oil (formula below)
St. Expedite Incense (formula below)
Glass of Water

After St. Expedite grants your request, you will need the following:

Large plate
Pound cake
3 Coins
Red, white or yellow candle

Dress your altar with the cloth. Obtain a St. Expedite prayer card or statue and a red, yellow or white candle. Alternatively, use a 7-day St. Expedite candle. On a piece of paper, write out your very specific request to St. Expedite in the form of a letter.

Anoint the candle with St. Expedite Oil. If you are using a 7-day candle, use a pointed object like a knife or screwdriver to poke a hole in the top of the candle and pour several drops of St. Expedite Oil into it.

St. Expedite Oil

1/4 cup Almond oil
9 drops Allspice oil
9 drops Sandalwood oil
9 drops Honeysuckle oil
3 Allspice berries

Place a glass of water upon the altar next to the image. Burn a little St. Expedite Incense on your altar as you recite your prayer and petition to St. Expedite. The following is an example:

"O St. Expedite, I conjure your presence and power with complete trust and confidence that you will do your duty for me in my time of need. [State your petition.] If you grant my request, I promise that I will make an offering to you in the form of [insert a description of your offering]. O St. Expedite, whose speed is unsurpassed, grant my petition fast, fast, fast!"

St. Expedite Incense

Combine equal parts of the following herbs and pulverize them:

Allspice powder
Sandalwood resin
Honeysuckle dried

Anoint the edges of the petition paper with a few drops of St. Expedite Oil. Then, fold it toward you a couple of times and place it beneath the image of St. Expedite. Light the candle and allow it to burn down completely.

Do not make your final offering to St. Expedite until he has completed the task you have assigned to him because if he receives his payment beforehand, he will assume that the request was fulfilled.

The typical offering to St. Expedite is a pound cake and a promise to tell, at least, one other person about his power. Only after he has granted your request, you should bring a pound cake and place it upon his altar. Arrange three coins in the form of a triangle on the plate that holds the pound cake, which can be homemade or purchased. Place a red, white or yellow candle in the center of the cake, light it and allow it to burn down. Afterward, you must tell, at least, one other person that St. Expedite has granted a request for you.

St. Expedite, also, accepts offerings of candy, flowers, liquor and Cinnamon. After the operation is completed, your request is fulfilled and you have kept your end of the bargain, take the refuse from this spell and place it a crossroad along with the pound cake.

St. Joseph

Call upon St. Joseph to improve your finances or to help you sell your house. He is the saint of builders. His feast day is March 19th, his day of the week is Sunday and his colors are red, white or gold.

Recite a prayer to St. Joseph as follows:

"O most glorious St. Joseph, I ask thee to intercede for me and whisper in the ear of the Lord, so that I may find relief from all of my present difficulties. I ask for protection for my home and business that I always have all that I need to keep a roof over my head and food on my table. Please, assist me with thy prayers to the Lord. [Insert your petition.] Amen."

St. Jude

St. Jude is widely called upon by people around the world, although, he is no longer an official saint of the Catholic church. St. Jude helps in desperate cases where quick solutions to a problem are needed.

He is well-known for performing financial miracles, however, he also helps break addictions and free prisoners, so he may be petitioned if you are in a work situation that makes you feel trapped. You must promise to promote devotion to him once your wish is granted by spreading his fame.

His day is October 28th, his day of the week is Sunday and his colors are green, white or red. The herb Rue is commonly used in spells requesting favors from him.

Anoint a green or white candle, preferably a St. Jude 7-day candle, with Rue oil and speak to St. Jude as follows:

"O Holy St. Jude, glorious apostle and faithful servant and friend of Jesus, pray for me that I may finally receive the consolation and succor of Heaven in all my necessities, tribulations and sufferings, in particular, [insert your petition] and that I may bless God with the elect throughout all eternity. Amen."

Place the paper with your hand-written petition underneath the candle and light it.

St. Lucy

St. Lucy of Syracuse was a noblewoman of the 3rd or 4th century who was said to have done remarkable things in the face of great adversity. Her name means "the light." She is the patron saint of the poor, salesmen, writers and of the eyes and vision.

Her feast day is December 13th. She is celebrated in different ways in many different countries, particularly those with a strong Lutheran population. Statues are made in her image and palm branches are used to symbolize her martyrdom. Plain little round cakes, sprinkled with confectioner's sugar or cupcakes decorated with icing to look like eyes, are made to celebrate the miracles she performed and are placed upon her altar as an offering. Celebrants sometimes wear a crown of lights in her honor.

Light a candle on your altar for St. Lucy. You may address her with this traditional prayer and ask for her assistance in matters pertaining to money, sales, writing or the health of your eyes as follows:

"O God, mercifully hear our prayers that as we venerate thy servant, St. Lucy, for the light of faith thou didst bestow upon her, thou wouldst vouchsafe to increase and to preserve this same light in our souls, that we may be able to avoid evil, to do good and to abhor nothing so much as the blindness and the darkness of evil and of sin. Relying on thy goodness, O God, we humbly ask thee, by the intersession of thy servant, St. Lucy that thou wouldst give perfect vision to our eyes, that they may serve for thy greater honor and glory, and for the salvation of our souls in this world, that we may come to the enjoyment of the unfailing light of the Lamb of God in paradise."

"St. Lucy, virgin and martyr, hear our prayers and obtain our petitions. [Insert your petition.] Amen."

Use the following oil to anoint your candles and make petitions to this saint:

St. Lucy Oil

1/4 cup Almond oil
7 drops Chamomile
7 drops Eyebright
7 drops Heliotrope

St. Martin Caballero

St. Martin Caballero or St. Martin of Tours is depicted as a Roman Centurion giving his cloak to a beggar. He is a calming presence and a very powerful saint who protects your home and helps you whenever you need money. When you are in need of help, light a candle and quickly petition him to provide you with a solution to your problem.

His day is November 11, his day of the week is Tuesday and his colors are red or white. He is not fussy about how he is addressed. If you have a problem, simply light a 7-day St. Martin candle and make your request. The solution will come swiftly.

St. Martin Caballero Oil

1/4 cup Almond oil
2 T. Brown Mustard seeds
2 T. Anise seeds
7 drops Cinnamon oil
7 drops Lavender oil

Crush the Mustard and Anise seeds and place them in a jar with a tightly fitting lid. Then, add the oils. Allow this mixture to remain in a warm place out of direct sunlight for two weeks, after which you may strain the seeds from the potion and place the liquid in a bottle with a lid.

Santa Muerte or Holy Death

Santa Muerte is a Mexican folk saint and an extremely powerful guardian who will be very aggressive with your enemies. She is commonly associated with the ancient Nahuatl Indian goddess whose name is Micteacacihuatl, although there are similar death goddesses throughout ancient Mexico and there is a long history of a similar spirits in Europe and the Middle East. She has enjoyed a resurgence in popularity in the past several years as the injustices in Mexico have intensified. You may find statues, candles and other items devoted to her at your local Mexican grocery store, botanica, metaphysical store or online.

At first glance, she looks like the scythe-wielding grim reaper with a white, skeletal face and a hooded robe. She holds the earth as a symbol of her worldly power in one hand and the scales of justice in the other. The original Aztec goddess was associated with the owl, which is, sometimes represented on images of her. The owl is, also, associated with Athena, Lilith, Ishtar and other goddesses of the underworld and those associated with rebellion and war. In Mexico, the owl is often regarded as a bad omen and is associated with witchcraft.

Santa Muerte is not recognized as a saint by the Catholic Church, but she is considered to be the mother of all. You can ask anything whatsoever of her and she will not pass judgment on your request. She is very powerful, but she requires devotion.

Whenever you work with Santa Muerte, make a small offering to her. She gladly accepts cigarettes, Tequila or other alcoholic beverages, fruit, flowers, cookies and candy. Sometimes petitioners smoke a cigarette with her and blow the smoke in her face or hold the cigarette so that the smoke streams upward into it. Always place a glass of water on the altar next to her image. You may offer her anything you like, as long as it comes from your heart. Lay it on the altar before her image, light a candle in her honor and ask for the cloak of her protection to be placed over you.

To petition her for relief from financial problems and for good luck, use a dark yellow candle, dress her statue and her altar in gold and offer her money or coins.

If your problem pertains to legal matters or contracts, use a green candle and a green altar cloth.

If you are having difficulties with someone at work, such as a boss, co-worker or a competition business, use a black candle and a black altar cloth and make an offering of cigarettes or alcohol. Pray to her and ask for protection from your enemies.

You may speak aloud to her or write out your petition and place it under a candle on an altar devoted to her. Allow this altar to become a place of power, where you make small offerings and prayers to her. Her altar will soon become a source of comfort and strength, where you can go to appeal to her for help in any matter.

For very difficult matters, pray a novena to her by lighting a candle upon her altar over the course of nine consecutive nights.

You may address her anyway you like. The following is only a suggestion:

"O Most Holy Death, I summon you to this place. Enlighten my home with your holy presence and place your cloak of protection over me. I ask that you break and destroy any curses that may have been placed upon me and release me from all envy and hatred. Bless me with love, prosperity, good health and [insert your petition]. Bless all those who live in my home with peace, health and well-being. Destroy all of my enemies, both great and small, and any who would harm me or my interests. O Most Holy Death, my beloved, you are my guardian and protector. Stay with me always and never forsake me all the days of my life. Amen."

Santa Muerte is very calming to work with and produces a very powerful, almost palpable energy when she is invoked. She will help you realize all of your ambitions and will mercilessly deal with your foes.

St. Patrick

St. Patrick is the patron saint of Ireland who provides good luck, prosperity and guidance. His Feast Day is March 17th. His day of the week is Sunday, his colors are green and white and his symbol is a shamrock.

St. Patrick is known for his intolerance of slavery, having escaped bondage himself. During his life, he denounced the mistreatment of others. If you feel enslaved by your current employment situation and wish to be free of it so you can do greater things with your life, petition St. Patrick for assistance and guidance.

Light a candle and make a petition to him using the following simple prayer:

"O Holy St. Patrick, illuminate and guide me. Release me from all forms of bondage and enslavement. Amen."

St. Peter

St. Peter helps remove obstacles and brings good fortune and better business. His day is June 29, his day of the week is Tuesday and his colors are red and white. He is a liberator who holds the Keys to the Kingdom, therefore, his symbol is two crossed keys.

Much like St. Patrick, he symbolizes freedom from enslavement and holds the keys to a happier more fulfilling life. Appeal to St. Peter to free you from financial bondage and lead you to a better life.

Pray to St. Peter as follows:

"Oh, Holy St. Peter, whom God has given the power to bind and loose, grant that we may be delivered from all evil and oppression through your loving intercession. Amen."

St. Philomena

The name, "Philomena," means "daughter of illumination." St. Philomena was only 13-years old when she was martyred. In her lifetime, she overcame all of the tortures and obstacles placed before her and was miraculously healed and restored.

Her feast day is August 13th, her day of the week is Saturday and her colors are pink and green. Although, sometimes orange and white are worn to honor her. Her symbols are an anchor, palm branches, arrows and a crown of flowers.

Those who venerate her and request her intercession find her to be extremely reliable and there are no limits to her ability to help you with any problem you have. Ask for her help with money problems, decision-making, illness or difficulties in your home, whether the problems are small or large.

St. Simon

St. Simon, also, called San Maximon or Hermano Simon, is a Guatemalan folk saint who grants the desires of his devotees without reservation. He was once called simply "Mam," which means "ancient one." He is a spirit of the crossroad who has the power to open the road to success in any endeavor. He is a saint of drunkards and gamblers and has a great deal of sexual energy.

He is usually portrayed as a mustached, Spanish-looking man seated in a chair, wearing a black suit and a hat, holding a bag of money in his left hand and a staff in his right.

To work with St. Simon, obtain an image of him and give him offerings of burning candles, cigarettes, cigars, corn tortillas and liquor. He prefers a type of Guatemalan drink known as Aguardiente.

Use the following color correspondences when working with St. Simon:

Black: For revenge and protection from enemies
Blue: Luck; gambling and employment
Green: Business and prosperity
Light blue or sky blue: Money and travel
White: To protect children
Yellow: Money; gambling; to improve business and to protect adults

Invoke St. Simon as follows:

"Infinite thanks to my brother, Simon, who always listens and never forgets me. Please, grant me [insert your petition]. You shall dwell in my heart and your name shall live forever and ever, my blessed brother Simon."

Use the following oil to anoint your candles and make petitions to this saint:

St. Simon Oil

1/4 cup Almond oil
3 drops Orange oil
3 drops Lemongrass oil
3 drops Spikenard (or Citronella) oil

Help from the Orishas

The Orishas or the African Powers are the ancestral spirits of the Yoruba-speaking people of West Africa. They are very powerful spirits who are willing to help those who call upon them with a sincere heart.

In Afro-Caribbean spiritualism, many of them are syncretic with specific Catholic saints and other gods and goddesses from pantheons worldwide. Much like the saints, they require devotion, so if you choose to work with any of them, give them their own altar or a special place in your home.

Eleggua

Eleggua (Eshu) is the key African Power who is called upon first in any spiritual working to ensure that the way is cleared. Eleggua is a messenger between the world of the living and the world of spirits. He is a spirit of the crossroad and a protector of travelers who presides over both good and bad fortune.

Like the Hindu Lord Ganesha, he is a road opener. Syncretically, he corresponds to the Haitian Vodou spirit Papa Legba and is associated with the Catholic saints Santo Niño de Atocha and St. Anthony who are both strong protectors. He is often employed to guard the entry way to people's homes from negativity.

Eleggua's day of the week is Monday, his colors are red and black and his sacred number is three. Dress his altar in red and black. Offer him rum, three-leafed Clovers and candy.

Use this ritual to appeal to Eleggua.

You will need the following:

Image of Eleggua (a head with cowrie shells or image on paper)
Red, white or black candle
Needle or thorn with which to make an inscription
Piece of paper
Eleggua Obstacle Breaker Oil, Eleggua Money Oil or Eleggua Job Oil (formulas below)
Red handkerchief or cloth
3 Peanuts
3 New Copper coins
Honey
Rum or other offerings
Red or black cord, yarn or string

Obtain an image or create a statue of Eleggua from a ball of clay and cowrie shells. He is portrayed as a man with a large head whose eyes, nose, mouth and ears are marked by a total of six shells.

Place your offering of rum upon the altar. Inscribe your name on the candle along with a short phrase that represents your desires. Anoint the candle with an oil formula according to your needs. Write your petition on a piece of paper.

Make the following prayer to Eleggua:

Prayer to the Orisha Eleggua

"Eleggua, open the door! Eleggua, open the door!
Remove every obstacle from my path,
So that I may succeed in my all my goals and objectives [insert your petition],
I will give praise and thanks to the gods."

Place the paper under the candle. Place the peanuts and the coins into the handkerchief. Add a few drops of Honey and a sprinkle of Rum. Tie it into a little bag with the cord and place it next to the candle.

Light the candle and when it has burned down, pass the handkerchief over your forehead, your heart and other chakra centers as you feel inclined. The purpose is to make an energetic bond between yourself and the items in the handkerchief.

Then, go to a four-way crossroad, stand holding the handkerchief up in both hands as an offering to Eleggua, first facing east, then west, then north and finally south. Then, toss the handkerchief into the crossroad and walk away without looking back.

Eleggua Obstacle Breaker Oil
(To clear obstacles)

1/2 cup Almond oil
2 T. Coffee grounds
1 tsp. Saltpeter
3 drops Coconut oil
3 drops Palm oil
Pinch of Sugar
Pinch of dirt from a 4-way crossroad
15 drops Rum

Use this oil in road opening prayers to Eleggua.

Eleggua Money Oil
(To attract money)

1/2 cup of Almond oil
7 drops Coconut oil
1 drop Peppermint oil
3 drops Sassafras oil

Eleggua Job Oil
(To obtain employment)

1/2 cup of Almond oil
6 drops Coconut oil
2 drop Anise oil
4 drops Orris oil

To protect yourself from robbery and violence when traveling for business or pleasure, carry on your person a red or black bag containing a few coffee beans and a whistle anointed with Eleggua Money Oil, Eleggua Job Oil or plain Coconut oil.

In honor of Eleggua string a beaded necklace as follows: Begin with three red beads, then add three black beads, then three more red beads and so on until you have strung 21 beads. Consecrate this special necklace to Eleggua and wear it for protection and good luck.

Ogun

Ogun (pronounced like "o-goon") is a fierce protector of the people. He is often portrayed as powerfully-built warrior, wearing a tribal mask and wielding a machete in one hand. But, he is more than just a warrior, he is a hunter and healer who gave people the knowledge of herbs. He is a guardian of orphans and both a path finder and a path maker, who serves as a strong, knowledgeable guide to those he protects. As a god of war, he is a skilled maker of weapons who works with iron, therefore, he is often represented hammering on an anvil. He can be belligerent when provoked, but he never turns his rage on his own people. Syncretically, he is associated with St. George the Dragonslayer.

Some historians credit the cult of Ogun with the success of the Haitian Revolution of 1804, which is the only documented successful uprising against slavery. Unquestionably, it was an Ogun-like spirit that came over the people and brought them to victory over their French oppressors.

Pray to Ogun for success in business, help finding a job and all of the aspects of being a warrior in today's modern world. Let his fiery energy inspire you to take vigorous action. Because he despises tyranny and oppression, he is a valuable ally to anyone who is trying to make his or her way in the corporate world.

He is a god of transitions. When there seems to be no way to do something, he makes a way. Ask him for help finding your way out of difficult situations and to better opportunities. He will use his machete to cut a path for you.

Ogun is associated with Mars because of his fiery, active nature, therefore, his day of the week is Tuesday. His colors are green, black and red and his symbols are iron, an anvil, a machete and two keys. His companion is a black dog. His sacred number is three and he enjoys rum, cigars and smoked fish as offerings upon his altar.

Anoint a candle with Ogun Lucky Oil and make your petition to him in writing or aloud.

Ogun Lucky Oil

1/2 cup of Almond oil
3 drops Coconut oil
1 drop Nutmeg oil
5 drops Strawberry oil
1 drop Sweet Pea oil

Ogun is an earth lord, therefore, after performing any ritual or spell involving him, bury the remains in the earth as a tribute to him.

The Seven African Powers

The Seven African Powers are a selection of seven very powerful gods from the pantheon of the Yoruba-speaking people. Eleggua, Obatala, Yemaya, Oshun, Oya, Chango and Ogun are commonly portrayed on prayer cards and 7-day candles with depictions of their heads and torsos arranged in a semi-circle around Christ the Just Judge, a ladder, a rooster and other symbolic images.

The African gods are powerful, primal and nonjudgmental. Since all human ancestral lines reach back to an ancient mother in Africa, everyone should feel free to work with these spirits. If they respond to you, then you can establish a deeper relationship with them.

To call upon these powerful spirits for help in any area of your life, obtain a Seven African Powers candle, anoint it with Seven African Powers Oil and recite the following prayer:

"O, Seven African Powers! O, Great Spirits, hear my petition and grant me peace and prosperity. [Make your request.] Let it be so! Amen."

Seven African Powers Oil

1/2 cup Safflower oil
1 T. Coconut oil
7 drops Allspice oil
7 drops Ambrosia oil
7 drops Cinnamon oil
7drops Lemon oil
7 drops Palma Christi oil
7 drops Peppermint oil
7 drops Sandalwood oil
7drops Vanilla oil
7 drops White Musk oil

Gods and Goddesses of Abundance

As you perform your spells, you may ask for added power and assistance from any number of deities associated with money and wealth. These gods and goddesses come from many places in the world and are of different natures. Some may be the spirits of ancient kings or queens, great men and women of renown, ascended masters, angelic beings or long forgotten ancestors. Some are a combination of spirits. Many of these are so old that little is known about them beyond their names and few small details.

In cases where there are known associations, such as animals, colors, days or herbs, incorporate this information into your request for aide from them. For example, when deities are associated with a particular animal, objects or color, include representations of such things on your altar when you make your invocation.

Abundantia: Greek goddess who brings wealth during sleep. She distributes food and money to people from her cornucopia.

Aje: West African (Yoruba) earth goddess of prosperity and wealth who appears as a bird scratching at the earth.

Anayaroli: East African (Temne) god or demon who rules over rivers and wealth.

Ashiakle: West African (Ghana) goddess of prosperity and wealth who was formed in the ocean. She is associated with cats and the colors red and white.

Cernunnos: Celtic horned god of wealth and abundance. He is associated with aspects of the Green Man motif in legend and literature, who is a spirit of the forests and nature.

Copia: Roman goddess of prosperity and opportunity. Her cornucopia is a goat's horn, from which she offers abundance and wealth.

Cronus: Greek god, also, known as Father Time who is the overseer of planting and harvest and a god of prosperity and abundance.

Danu: Celtic mother goddess of material wealth, prosperity, creativity and strength. She is associated with the north and water. The Danube River is named for her.

Dedun: A Nubian and later an Egyptian god of prosperity and wealth who is associated with incense.

Dzambhala: A Chinese deity who is an aspect of Buddha. He is related to the Hindu god Kuber and like the goddess Tara, he has many aspects represented as colors. Yellow Dzambhala is the Buddha of wealth who produces precious jewels from his lips. Like Kuber he is sometimes represented with a mongoose.

Fortuna: Roman goddess of abundance, luck and fate.

Frey: Norse god of prosperity. His day is Friday.

Freya: Norse goddess of fertility, abundance and success in war. She is the wife of Frey, her symbol is a cat and her day is, also, Friday.

Frigg: Norse mother goddess of enrichment, abundance, protection and creativity. Her day is Friday and the apple is sacred to her.

Habondia: Celtic witch goddess of fertility and abundance who has been mostly forgotten and absorbed by other goddesses such as Brigid. It seems she may have once been associated with Cernunnos or a similar god of the forest. Honor Habondia with plants, flowers and symbols of a bountiful harvest.

Use the following oil in your spells, prayers and petitions to Habondia for abundant wealth:

Habondia Oil

1/4 cup Grapeseed oil
3 drops Agrimony oil
3 drops Calendula oil
3 drops Chamomile oil
7 drops Gold of Pleasure oil (Camelina or False Flax)

Hades: Greek god of death and prosperity.

Hecate: Greek goddess of regeneration, transformation, wealth, prosperity and decision-making.

Horus: Egyptian god of success.

Kubera: Hindu god of money, prosperity and wealth who is Treasurer of the Gods. He is associated with a mongoose. The following is a Sanskrit mantra dedicated to Lord Kubera, the Hindu god of money. His mantra is: "Om Shreem Om Hreem Shreem Hreem Kleem Shreem Kleem Vitteswaraay Namah."

The first nine words are pronounced exactly as you see them, however, the last two are pronounced like "Vit-es-wah-ray-yah Na-mah-hah."

Lakshmi (Lax-shi-me): Hindu goddess of wealth and abundance whose name is derived from a Sanskrit word meaning goal or aim. Her mantra for abundance is: "Om Shreem Maha Lakshmiyei Swaha." It is pronounced: "Aum Shreem Ma-hah Lax-she-me-yea Swah-hah."

Mercury: Roman god of communication and commerce. He is the god of merchants and travelers, which is why Mercury head dimes are the preferred coins used in some money spells. He may be likened to the Greek god Hermes and the Celtic god Toutatis or Teutates. Toutatis is associated with the Hazel tree and Hazel nuts

Moneta: Roman goddess of wealth who dispenses good advice.

Nanna: Norse goddess of wisdom, fertility, abundance, prosperity and wealth.

Odin: Norse All-father and god of protection, knowledge, abundance, wealth, creativity and inspiration.

Osanobua: West African creator and father god who grants healing, prosperity and wealth. He is associated with silver coins and the toucan.

Pluto: Roman God of the Underworld and of rich land, plentiful harvests and abundant wealth. According to legend, sacrifices of wreaths made of Narcissus, Maidenhair and Cypress were made to him.

Renenutet: Egyptian goddess of nourishment, wealth and plentiful harvest to whom sacrifices were once performed to ensure bounty. She is associated with the cobra and is sometimes depicted as a woman with a cobra's head.

Rosemerta: Gaelic and Celtic goddess of fertility and wealth. Her symbols are a cornucopia, a double-bladed axe and a stick with two snakes intertwined.

Saubhagya-Bhuvanesvari: Buddhist goddess of good luck, fortune and prosperity.

Sors: Roman god of luck. Begin your petition to him with the phrase, "Sors, guide my arrow."

Tara: A Hindu and Buddhist goddess who may be regarded as a feminine form of Buddha. She represents success through hard work and achievement. Tara has many different colors with different aspects of her powers. Yellow Tara is associated with prosperity. Her main mantra is: "Om Tare Tuttare Ture Swaha." It is pronounced: "Aum Too-tar-ay Too-ray Swah-hah."

Thalia: One of the three Greek Charities or Graces. Her name means abundance and luxury.

Tsai Shen: Chinese god of wealth who is honored in the New Year. He is often depicted riding a black tiger.

Wamala: East African god of prosperity and wealth.

14 HERBS AND FOODS FOR HEALTH, WEALTH AND WISDOM

There is far more than just superstition behind the associations of certain herbs and foods with health, wealth and wisdom. Some herbs and foods not only bring wealth vibrations into your life through the magic of spells, but supply your body with energy, improve circulation and provide necessary nutrition to your brain and other organs. They keep your life energy level high and heighten your spiritual connection.

You are wise to learn about herbs and foods that help you to have the good health and stamina to earn more money and enjoy the fruits of your labor. Understanding their physical and metaphysical properties helps you focus your intention and enhance their ability to bring you prosperity.

As you enjoy the following healthy foods, consider the particular magical properties they bring into your life.

In magical formulas, Coconut is used to drive away bad spirits and to bring good luck and good health. In the West, the Coconut is conventionally thought of as a tasty summer treat or the topping for cakes and desserts. But, it has much broader use in the East where the entire tree is used in the service of mankind's physical and spiritual health. In southeast Asia, the Coconut is known as the "tree of life," because it is so versatile. According to experts, the oil of the Coconut has powerful anti-viral and anti-bacterial properties. It is used internally and topically to heal lesions and other kinds of inflammation. It supports healthy glandular function and cooking with Coconut oil may help you to lose weight and feel more energetic. The list of healing benefits of the Coconut is seemingly endless and it has no known toxicity or contraindications of use.

Sea Buckthorn, sometimes called simply Buckthorn, is gaining popularity as a superfood because its fruit is loaded with vitamins and amino acids. This small, orange fruit helps protect the body from the damaging effects of too much physical stress.[20] It encourages the growth of healthy brain tissue, improves memory and encourages cell repair and healthy cell regeneration. Magically, it is used to guard against evil spirits and black magic, as an aid in court cases, contracts and legal matters and to make wishes come true. Keep these benefits in mind as you eat these tart, flavorful berries in autumn when they ripen or enjoy the benefits year round with Sea Buckthorn seed extract, which is available at health food stores.

Purslane, which is used in some spells for prosperity and to recover money owed, is, also, a highly nutritious plant. It is a major source of Omega 3 fatty acids, which help in fighting depression and other common mental disorders. Fresh Purslane is a delicious addition to salads, stir-fry and other dishes. It can, also, be taken as a tea. Moreover, the entire plant including the vine may be eaten cooked or raw.

Onions are used to cleanse, purify, strengthen and to draw money. They are a very helpful food for people who suffer from extreme stress that puts a lot of strain on the adrenal glands and leaves them feeling exhausted and unable to recover even after a long sleep. In such cases, an onion or two per day can help revitalize the glandular system and restore vigor. Although, those taking pharmaceutical blood thinners should take caution because eating too many onions can cause the blood to thin.

Cucumbers are used in spells to help the seeds of

prosperity you plant in your life to expand, grow and bear fruit. Peas represent coins and are used to draw money, but they, also, contain Vitamin K and manganese. Cabbage is a traditional food for good luck, but it, also, contains Vitamins C and K. According to many researchers, Vitamin K is good for healthy veins, may help increase bone density and protect against osteoporosis, which is a health problem for both women and men.

To make a healthy, money and wealth drawing salad, toss together fresh Purslane, Onions, Cucumbers, Peas and Cabbage. Add a tablespoon of money-drawing Flax seed oil as a dressing for even more mentally balancing and mood-lifting Omega fatty acids.

Are you hoping to get a raise? Then, top off your salad with some fresh Fenugreek sprouts. Besides bringing money and good luck, Fenugreek is beneficial to the glandular system and helps fight colds and flu.

Alfalfa is used in spells and potions to promote good luck and prevent poverty. It is rich in vitamins, trace minerals and protein. It is a valuable herb for detoxifying the system from harmful metals like mercury and lead, which can lead to extreme fatigue and serious health problems. Sprout your own Alfalfa seeds to maximize their benefits.

Good Fortune and Prosperity in the New Year

New Year's Eve is a time when people think about their hopes and dreams of prosperity and financial abundance in the new year. In Mexico, prosperity in the coming year is contemplated just after midnight in the first few minutes of New Year's Day. At this time, it is customary to eat twelve Grapes, one by one, while thinking about a wish or hope for each month of the coming year as you do so.

There are similar customs in other Spanish-speaking countries with a variation that includes eating one of the twelve Grapes for each chime of the clock on New Year's Eve. Grapes are highly nutritious and contain antioxidants and Resveratrol, which is linked to longevity in studies.

Grapes and their leaves are, also, used in spells for money, fertility and abundance.

Around the world, pomegranate seeds are a symbol of good luck. In China they are eaten on New Year's Day to ensure good fortune in the coming year. But, Pomegranate seeds and their juice are, also, full of anti-oxidants, help lower LDL "bad" cholesterol and fight heart disease and cancer. This is a very lucky fruit, indeed, for stressed out executives, salesmen and entrepreneurs.

In the south and some areas of the mid-western United States, it is customary to eat Black-eyed Peas as the first meal of the year to ensure a prosperous new year.

Traditions vary widely with regard to how the beans are prepared, what they are served with and when. Some people serve them just after midnight and others serve them as a traditional lunch meal on New Year's Day. Black-eyed Peas are often eaten with Cornbread and Cabbage or other leafy green vegetables. Some people even add coins to the soup pot. In this yearly ritual, Black-eyed Peas represent coins, the green vegetables represent cash and Cornbread represents bars of gold.

Black-eyed Peas

The following recipe may be cooked in a crock pot or on the stove top.

Ingredients:

1 Lb. Black-eyed Peas, dried
1 Onion, chopped
1 Garlic clove, finely chopped
1 Bay leaf
1 tsp. Thyme
6 cups Water
1/2 to 1 tsp. Sea Salt
1 to 2 tsp. Chili Powder (optional)

Directions:

Begin by soaking a pound of dried Black-eyed Peas overnight. Carefully sift through the beans and discard any debris, taking special care to search for any tiny rock fragments. Rinse them in a colander and place them in a bowl. Cover them with enough water for them to absorb and expand. Allow them to soak overnight or for, at least, six hours.

Afterward, strain the beans. Combine the above ingredients. Place them in a crock pot set on "high" for 3 1/2 hours. Or, cook them covered on the stove top by bringing them to a boil and then reducing the heat to a simmer for 2 to 3 hours or until the Black-eyed Peas are tender. Add water as necessary.

This recipe yields approximately 6 cups.

Sweet Cornbread

A recipe similar to this one is made and eaten with meals year round throughout the U.S. and Mexico. Corn is a plant sacred to numerous gods and goddesses among the Mayans, the Aztecs, the Pawnee and other Indian tribes on the North American Continent. Corn is seen as the origin of the life force, itself.

Cornbread should always be broken and buttered and never cut with a knife to maintain good fortune.

Ingredients:

1 cup White Flour
1 cup Yellow Cornmeal
1/3 cup White Sugar
1/3 cup Brown Sugar
1 tsp. Sea Salt
3 1/2 tsp. Baking Powder
1 Egg
1 cup Milk
1/3 cup Olive, Grapeseed or Sunflower oil

Directions:

Preheat the oven to 400 degrees F (200 degrees C). In a large bowl, combine the dry ingredients and blend them. Then, stir in the egg, milk and oil. Blend this batter until it is free of large lumps. Pour the batter into a greased 11" x 7" baking dish.

Bake at 400 degrees for 20 to 25 minutes or until a toothpick inserted into the middle comes out clean. Cut the bread into little golden squares and serve them with butter.

Magical Culinary Herbs and Teas

Hyssop is used in magical formulas to draw helpful spirits and reverse bad luck, however, it is, also, a highly nutritious herb that eases difficult breathing and soothes away sore throats and other symptoms of being run down. Whenever you overdo it at work, brew a cup of soothing, lucky Hyssop tea by placing a small handful of dried Hyssop blossoms into a small pot of boiling water.

Basil is a valuable herb for spiritual healing and protection. It is used by Mexican curanderos who perform the traditional Limpia (cleansing) with a large bundle of the fresh herb in their hands. This practice serves to drive away adverse energies and protects the healer from contamination. Basil is used in magical formulas for protection, wealth and success in business endeavors. But, Basil is, also, a valuable healing herb to use when you have overworked yourself and are beginning to feel a little run down or on the verge of "catching something." Add dried Basil to soups, make a tea or inhale the essential oil to receive the benefits of this herb.

Bay leaf is used in magical formulas for protection, purification and in spells to make prayers and petitions. It is, also, a powerful herb for fighting cold and allergy symptoms, dissipating congestion and improving respiration. Nicholas Culpeper's description of the properties of the Bay tree is powerful and acknowledges both its physical and metaphysical properties. He says, it "resisteth witchcraft very potently, as also all the evils old Saturn can do to the body." Further, he says, "neither witch nor devil, thunder nor lightning, will hurt a man in the place where a bay-tree is."[21] Use bay leaf to season broth and as a tea.

Ginger root is used in spells and formulas designed to draw money, power and success. But, it is, also, a valuable sleep aide and a natural source of melatonin. Melatonin not only helps you to sleep better when you are suffering from stress or anxiety, but it is one of the chemicals needed by the pineal gland, your source of dreams and inspiration, to function properly. Along with helping to increase your intuition, Ginger is good for treating dizziness, indigestion and nausea, as well.

Pine needles are used in spells for protection and money drawing. Strawberry leaves are used in spells for good luck. Both are excellent sources phytonutrients. Make a healthy tea with a handful of freshly gathered Pine needles and Strawberry leaves for good luck, prosperity and lots of Vitamin C, which helps keep you energized, healthy and clear-headed.

Lemon Balm is used in potions and spells for success, however, it is, also, a natural nerve-calming agent and powerful anti-viral, which may be of help to you if you feel you are coming down with a cold or flu.

Coltsfoot is a major herb in Hoodoo money drawing formulas. As a healing tea, it is useful for fighting asthma, allergies, colds and congestion.

Vervain and Chamomile are money and luck drawing herbs. Both are nutritious and help maintain good health and calm focus. Vervain has benefits to the liver and the digestive system. Chamomile is well-known for its calming powers and is a natural pain reliever and digestion soother. Make a cup of either of these teas or combine them in one brew.

Brew a cup of Money Drawing Tea: Place a handful each of Basil and Bay leaf into a pot of boiling water. Add a tablespoon of dried or fresh Ginger and Lemon juice or

Lemon peels for added nutrients and a pleasant flavor.

Fight stress and anxiety with a cup of Success Tea: Add a tablespoon each of Lemon Balm and Coltsfoot in approximately one cup of boiling water. Add a little Ginger root, raw, dried or powdered for added calming and healing power. This is an excellent tea to take right before bed time to ensure a restful sleep and fight off colds and respiratory problems.

Incorporate your intention to draw money and wealth into your preparation and consumption of these foods and beverages to heighten their natural powers.

As you consume other healthy, wealthy herbs and foods, remember their magical powers. The next time you eat an Almond or a Cashew, keep in mind the money and prosperity drawing powers of each of them. Whenever you enjoy heart-healthy oatmeal, envision its money drawing power bringing riches to you. Our wise ancestors knew about these things and it is important for us to remember them.

LIST OF MEASUREMENT CONVERSIONS
AND ABBREVIATIONS

Abbreviation Key for Measurements

T. = Tablespoon
tsp. = teaspoon
oz. = ounce
g = gram
ml = milliliter

Conversion of Measurements

3 tsp. = 1 T.
1 cup = 16 T.
1 cup = 8 oz.
1 pint =16 oz.
1 pint – 2 cups
1 tsp. = approximately 4.2 g
1 cup liquid = approximately 220 to 240 g
1 cup non-liquid = approximately 120 to 140 g
1 dram = 1/8 oz. = 60 grams = 3.697 ml = 60 drops
1 dram = .125 fl. oz. or approximately 3/4 tsp.
1 pint = approximately 473 ml
1 ml = 15 drops of liquid

GLOSSARY

Altar: Work space. A place set aside for magical workings.

Amulet: A charm or talisman.

Anoint: To apply oil to a person or object.

Botanica: A metaphysical store that specializes in products common to Spanish-speaking countries.

Censer: Thurible or incense burner.

Charge: The act of infusing an object with elemental energy.

Charms: Objects intended to bring good fortune and protect from evil.

Conjure: To call upon; to invoke or manifest.

Crossed: The condition of having an accumulation of negative energy.

Curse: A malefic spell intended to do grave harm.

Divination: A method of obtaining information about the past, present or future.

Dress: To anoint an object; to apply oil to a candle, talisman or other object.

Feed: To energize and maintain the energy of a magical object or familiar spirit to keep it alive.

Glory Be Prayer: "Glory be to the Father and to the Son and to the Holy Spirit, as it was in the beginning, is now and ever shall be, world without end. Amen."

Golem: A spiritual being created to act as a servant. Also, called a servitor or a familiar spirit.

Grimoire: A spell book.

Hail Mary Prayer: "Hail Mary, full of grace. Our Lord is with thee. Blessed art thou among women and blessed is the fruit of thy womb, Jesus. Holy Mary, Mother of God, pray for us sinners, now and at the hour of our death. Amen."

Hex: A spell, especially one intended to cause misfortune.

Hoodoo: A general term for American witchcraft practices originating in Africa and blended with Native American practices, Kabbalism and European folk magic.

Incantation: A chant or a mantra. Powerful words recited over an object to direct its energy.

Magic: The art and science of effecting change in the physical world by metaphysical means.

Mojo Bag: An approximately 2" by 3" flannel or cotton bag with a drawstring. A talisman or "hand" assembled to create a particular effect and regularly charged or fed.

Novena: A series of Catholic-style prayers conducted over the course of nine consecutive days.

Our Father Prayer: "Our Father which art in heaven, Hallowed be thy name. Thy kingdom come, Thy will be done in earth, as it is in heaven. Give us this day our daily bread. And forgive us our debts, as we forgive our debtors. And lead us not into temptation, but deliver us from evil: For thine is the kingdom, and the power, and the glory, for ever. Amen."

Personal Effects: Items that carry a person's unique, vibrational harmonic frequency. For example, blood, other bodily fluids, hair, underwear, signature or a photograph; also, called personal concerns.

Petition: A specific request made to a spirit, which is usually written down.

Poppet: An effigy or a doll. A representation of a person made of wax, cloth or other material.

Psalms: A book of the Old Testament, which is a powerful grimoire commonly used in American Hoodoo and Mexican Witchcraft.

Talisman: An amulet. An object that has magical powers.

Tetragrammaton: The four elements Kabbalistically expressed as "Yod He Vau He" and sometimes abbreviated as "JHVH." This concept was later anthropomorphized as "God" and his name is pronounced "Jehovah" or "Ya-weh" by Jews and Christians.

Thurible: Censer. An incense burner.

Uncrossing: A spell or ritual intended to reverse a crossed condition.

Voodoo: African-based spiritual and religious practices commonly found in New Orleans, Memphis and, historically, elsewhere in the mid-west and the south of the U.S. This American spelling is used to differentiate it from Haitian Vodou.

Wicca: A religion based on a form of initiatory witchcraft founded by Gerald Gardner in the 1950s. It is of two basic types: British Traditional Wicca and Neo-Wicca.

Witchcraft: A worldwide practice, which is based on esoteric scientific principles.

Work Space: An altar; a place where rituals or spells are conducted.

Working: A spell or ritual; also, called a "job" or "laying down a trick" in Hoodoo.

REFERENCES

1. Hurston, Zora Neale, "Mules and Men," 1935.

2. Ibid.

3. Ibid.

4. Leland, Charles G., "Aradia, Gospel of the Witches," 1899. Pp. 41-42.

5. Hyatt, Harry Middleton, "Folk-lore from Adams County, Illinois," 1935. Pp. 34-35.

6. Owen, Mary Alicia, "Old Rabbit the Voodoo, and other Sorcerers," London: T. Fisher Unwin, 1893.

7. Lawrence, Robert Means, "The Magic of the Horse-Shoe With Other Folk-Lore Notes," 1898. http://www.sacred-texts.com/etc/mhs/

8. Flight, Edward G., "The Horse Shoe: The True Legend of St. Dunstan and the Devil; Showing How the Horse-shoe Came to be a Charm Against Witchcraft," 3rd Edition, London,1871.

9. Leland, Charles G., "Etruscan Roman Remains in Popular Tradition," 1892. P. 364

10. Leland, Charles G., "Aradia, Gospel of the Witches," 1899. P. 23-24

11. Leland, Charles G., "Aradia, Gospel of the Witches," 1899. Pp. 25-27

12. Scheible, Johann and Joseph Ennemoser, Moses,"The sixth and seventh books of Moses: or, Moses' magical spirit-art, known as the wonderful arts of the old wise Hebrews, taken from the Mosaic books of the Cabala and the Talmud, for the good of mankind. Translated from the German, word for word, according to old writings," London, 1880.

13. Hurston, Zora Neale, "Mules and Men," 1935.

14. Godey, Louis Antoine and Sarah Josepha Buell Hale, Ed., "Godey's Lady's Book, Volume 56, 1858.

15. Bloomfield, Maurice, Transl. "Hymns of the Atharva-Veda, Sacred Books of the East, Vol. 42," 1897.

16. Ibid.

17. Mathers, MacGregor S.L., Trans., Aleister Crowley, Editing and Additional Material, "Lemegeton Clavicula Salomonis, The Lesser Key of Solomon," 1903.

18. Bardon, Franz, Trans. A. Radspieler, "Initiation Into Hermetics: A Course of Instruction of Magic Theory & Practice," Dieter Ruggeberg, 1971.

19. Hall, Manly P., "Secret Teachings of All Ages," 1928, P. 102. http://www.sacred-texts.com/eso/sta/index.htm

20. Zheng, Xianyun, Wenmin Long, Gening Liu, Xiaomin Zhang, Xiaolan Yang, "Journal of Science Food and Agriculture, "Effect of sea buckthorn (Hippophae rhamnoides ssp. sinensis) leaf extract on the swimming endurance and exhaustive exercise-induced oxidative stress of rats," Volume 92, Issue 4, pages 736–742, 15 March 2012. http://onlinelibrary.wiley.com/doi/10.1002/jsfa.4634/abstract

21. Culpeper, Nicholas. "Complete Herbal," 1653

OTHER WINTER TEMPEST BOOKS

If you enjoyed this book, you might enjoy other Winter Tempest Books:

All Natural Dental Remedies: Herbs and Home Remedies to Heal Your Teeth & Naturally Restore Tooth Enamel by Angela Kaelin

Black Magic for Dark Times: Spells of Revenge and Protection by Angela Kaelin

Blood and Black Roses: A Dark Bouquet of Vampires, Romance and Horror by Sophia diGregorio (Fiction)

The Forgotten: The Vampire Prince by Sophia diGregorio

How to Communicate with Spirits: Séances, Ouija Boards and Summoning by Angela Kaelin

How to Develop Advanced Psychic Abilities: Obtain Information about the Past, Present and Future Through Clairvoyance by Sophia diGregorio

How to Read the Tarot for Fun, Profit and Psychic

Development for Beginners and Advanced Readers by Angela Kaelin

How to Write Your Own Spells for Any Purpose and Make Them Work by Sophia diGregorio

Magical Healing: How to Use Your Mind to Heal Yourself and Others by Angela Kaelin

Natural Remedies for Reversing Gray Hair: Nutrition and Herbs for Anti-aging and Optimum Health by Thomas W. Xander

Practical Black Magic: How to Hex and Curse Your Enemies by Sophia diGregorio

To Conjure the Perfect Man by Sophia diGregorio (Fiction)

The Traditional Witches' Book of Love Spells by Angela Kaelin

Traditional Witches' Formulary and Potion-making Guide: Recipes for Magical Oils, Powders and Other Potions by Sophia diGregorio

Disclaimer: The author and publisher of this guide has used her best efforts in preparing this document. The author makes no representation or warranties with respect to the accuracy, applicability, fitness or completeness of the contents of this document. The author disclaims any warranties expressed or implied. The author of this book is not a medical or legal professional and is not qualified to give medical or legal advice. Nothing in this document should be construed as medical or legal advice. The material in this book is presented for informational purposes only. Nothing in this book should be construed as incitement to dangerous or illegal acts and the reader is advised to be aware of and heed all pertinent laws in his or her city, state, country or other jurisdiction. Any medical or legal questions should be addressed to the proper medical or legal authorities. The author shall in no event be held liable for any losses or damages, including but not limited to special, incidental, consequential or other damages incurred by the use of this information. The statements in this book have not been evaluated by any government organization. The statements contained herein represent the legally protected opinions of the author and are presented for informational purposes only. Anyone who uses any of the information in the book does so at their own risk with the understanding that the author cannot be held responsible for the consequences. This document contains material protected under copyright laws. Any unauthorized reprint, transmission or resale of this material without the express permission of the author is strictly prohibited.

FTC Disclaimer: The author has no connection to nor was paid by any brand or product described in this document with the exception of any other books mentioned which were written by the author or published by Winter Tempest Books.